PENGUIN BOOKS
FEAR AND FORGIVENESS

Harsh Mander is a social worker and writer. He was awarded the Rajiv Gandhi National Sadbhavana Award, and the M.A. Thomas National Human Rights Award in 2002. Harsh Mander is convenor of Aman Biradari, a people's campaign for secularism, peace and justice, and works for Nyayagrah, for legal justice and reconciliation for the survivors of the Gujarat 2002 carnage, and Dil Se, for the rights of homeless children, youth and women. He assists the Supreme Court in trying to ensure the right to food of all citizens.

A visiting professor in the Indian Institute of Management, Ahmedabad, he also writes columns for *The Hindu* and the *Hindustan Times*. His book, *Unheard Voices: Stories of Forgotten Lives*, was published by Penguin India in 2001.

Harsh Mander lives in Delhi with his wife and daughter.

Fear and Forgiveness
The Aftermath of Massacre

HARSH MANDER

PENGUIN BOOKS

An imprint of Penguin Random House

PENGUIN BOOKS

USA | Canada | UK | Ireland | Australia
New Zealand | India | South Africa | China | Singapore

Penguin Books is part of the Penguin Random House group of companies
whose addresses can be found at global.penguinrandomhouse.com

Published by Penguin Random House India Pvt. Ltd
4th Floor, Capital Tower 1, MG Road,
Gurugram 122 002, Haryana, India

Penguin
Random House
India

First published by Penguin Books India 2009

Copyright © Harsh Mander 2009

All rights reserved

10 9 8 7 6 5 4 3 2

The views and opinions expressed in this book are the author's own and the facts
are as reported by him which have been verified to the extent possible, and the
publishers are not in any way liable for the same.

ISBN 9780143102212

For sale in the Indian Subcontinent and Singapore only

Typeset in AGaramond by R. Ajith Kumar, New Delhi
Printed at Repro India Limited

This book is sold subject to the condition that it shall not, by way of trade
or otherwise, be lent, resold, hired out, or otherwise circulated without the
publisher's prior consent in any form of binding or cover other than that in
which it is published and without a similar condition including this condition
being imposed on the subsequent purchaser.

www.penguin.co.in

MIX
Paper from
responsible sources
FSC® C047271

This is a legitimate digitally printed version of the book and therefore might not
have certain extra finishing on the cover.

Dedicated to the many in Gujarat
who resisted the storms of hate and divide
with compassion and courage
Because of them, I can still hope

Contents

viii Contents

Prologue

Spring, 2002: a tempestuous storm of engineered sectarian hatred breaks out and rages for many months in Gujarat. Many parts of the prosperous state are convulsed by some of the most gruesome episodes of ethnic bloodletting that have sporadically scarred the country since its partition more than half a century ago. During many overcast days of shame and suffering, blood flows freely on the streets as tens of thousands of homes are razed to the ground. This gale of hate leaves in its wake the brutal murder, often by burning alive, of an estimated 2000 men, women and children, almost entirely of the Muslim community, and mass rapes and slaughter of young girls. More than 200,000 people flee in terror as their homes and livelihoods are systematically plundered and destroyed, reducing them to refugees in their own homeland.

However, this book, written over the past seven years, is not so much about the grim events of 2002 as a chronicle of the aftermath of the massacre, about the continuing climate of dread and loathing that pervades years after the storm passed, breached only by individual acts of compassion and courage, by a love that sustains amidst slaughter. The book explores the possibilities of forgiveness and reconciliation in times of fear and hate.

I must begin this record with my first essay on the carnage, written in the red heat of disbelief and anguish just days after it broke out. I was on a sabbatical from the civil service at the time, and was working with an international development agency. On reading what was described as a major Hindu–Muslim riot, I decided to travel to Ahmedabad, which was worst hit by the mass violence, and attempt to craft a response of humanitarian assistance. It was a journey that was to change the course of my life irrevocably.

I have seen and handled many riots as part of my duties in the Indian Administrative Service, but I was utterly stunned by what I saw and heard in the relief camps. I quickly realized that what the people of Gujarat had survived was not a savage riot, but a state-sponsored pogrom. The gruesome mass brutality—substantially targeted at women and children from the minority Muslim community—was systematically planned in advance and executed by right wing religious fundamentalist Hindutva groups. I grieved at the role and impunity of the state authorities, including my civil service colleagues, who had enabled, and in some instances actively abetted, the planned massacre and destruction. 'Cry, My Beloved Country', an article I wrote as a still-serving civil servant, was how I chose to share my grief and shock with my people. Though bitterly attacked by some, the article quickly circulated through the internet to far corners of the country and the world, was translated in many languages, and an edited version was published by the *Times of India*. I reproduce it as it was originally written.

> *Numbed with disgust and horror, I bear witness to the terror and massacre that convulsed the state of Gujarat. My heart is sickened, my soul wearied, my shoulders aching with the burdens of guilt and shame.*
> *Cry, my beloved country!*

As you walk through the camps of survivors of the massacre in Ahmedabad, in which an estimated one hundred thousand women, men, and children are huddled in nearly hundred make-shift temporary settlements, displays of overt grief are unusual. People clutch small bundles of relief materials, all that they now own in the world, with dry and glassy eyes. Some talk in low voices, others busy themselves with the tasks of everyday living in these most elementary of shelters, looking for food and milk for children, tending the wounds of the injured.

But once you sit anywhere in these camps, people begin to speak and their words are like masses of pus released by slitting large festering wounds. The horrors that they speak of are so macabre, that my pen falters in the writing. The pitiless brutality against women and small children by organized bands of armed young men is more savage than anything witnessed in the riots that have shamed this nation from time to time during the past century.

I force myself to write a small fraction of all that I heard and saw, because it is important that we all know. Or maybe I write also because I need to share my own burdens.

What can you say about a woman eight months pregnant who begged to be spared? Her assailants instead slit open her stomach, pulled out her foetus and slaughtered it before her eyes. What can you say about a family of nineteen being killed by flooding their house with water and then electrocuting them with high-tension electricity? What can you say?

What do you say to a small boy of six whom you hold in your lap, his eye gashed, his head bundled in bandages, as he describes in explicit detail about how his father, mother and six brothers and sisters were battered to death before his eyes? He survived only because he fell unconscious, and was taken for dead. How do you look in the eyes of the members of a family escaping from Naroda-Patiya, one of the worst-hit settlements in Ahmedabad, as they speak of losing a young woman and her three-month-old son, because a police constable directed her to 'safety' and she found herself instead surrounded by a mob which doused her with kerosene and set her and her baby on fire?

I have never known a riot which has used the sexual subjugation of women so widely as an instrument of violence as in the recent mass barbarity in Gujarat. There are reports everywhere of gang-rape, of young girls and women, often in the presence of members of their families, followed by their murder by burning alive, or by bludgeoning with a hammer and in one case with a screw driver. Women in the Aman Chowk shelter told appalling stories about how armed men disrobed themselves in front of a group of terrified women to cow them down further.

In Ahmedabad, most people I met—social workers, journalists, survivors—agree that what Gujarat witnessed after the tragic torching of the railway compartment in Godhra was not a riot, but a systematic, planned massacre, a pogrom. Everyone spoke of the pillage and plunder being organized like a military operation against an external armed enemy. An initial truck would arrive broadcasting inflammatory slogans, soon followed by more trucks which disgorged young men, mostly in khaki shorts and saffron sashes. They were armed with sophisticated explosive materials, country weapons, daggers and trishuls. They also carried water bottles, to sustain them in their exertions. The leaders were seen communicating on mobile telephones from the venues of the mass violence, receiving instructions from and reporting back to a co-ordinating centre. Some were seen with documents and computer sheets listing Muslim families and their properties. They had detailed precise knowledge about buildings and businesses held by members of the minority community, such as who were partners say in a restaurant business, or which Muslim homes had Hindu spouses who should be spared in the violence. This was not a spontaneous upsurge of mass anger. It was a meticulously planned genocide.

The trucks carried quantities of gas cylinders. Rich Muslim homes and business establishments were first systematically looted, stripped down of all their valuables, then cooking gas was released from cylinders into the buildings for several minutes. A trained member of the group then lit the flame that efficiently engulfed the building. In some cases, acetylene gas which is used for welding steel, was employed to explode large concrete buildings. Mosques and dargahs were razed, and were replaced by statues of Hanuman and saffron flags. Some dargahs in Ahmedabad city crossings have overnight been demolished and their sites covered with road building material, and bulldozed so efficiently that these spots are indistinguishable from the rest of the road. Traffic now plies over these former dargahs, as though they never existed.

The unconscionable failures and active connivance of the state police and administrative machinery is also now widely acknowledged. The police is known to have misguided people straight into the hands of rioting mobs. They provided protective shields to crowds bent on pillage, arson, rape and murder, and were deaf to the pleas of the desperate Muslim victims, many of them women and children. There have been many reports of police firing directly mostly at the minority community, which was the target of most of the mob violence. The large majority of arrests are also from the same community which was the main victim of the pogrom.

As one who has served in the Indian Administrative Service for over two decades, I feel great shame at the abdication of duty by the large majority of my peers in the civil and police administration. The law did not require *any of them to await orders from their political supervisors before they organized the decisive use of force to prevent the brutal escalation of violence, and to protect vulnerable women and children from the organized, murderous mobs. The law instead imposed on them the onerous responsibility to act independently, fearlessly, impartially, decisively, with courage and compassion. If even one official had so acted in the city of Ahmedabad, she or he could have used powers under the Criminal Procedure Code to deploy the police forces and call in the army, to halt the violence and protect the people in a matter of hours. The success of a few fine young police officers to quell the mass violence in their districts through rapid and non-partisan police action underlines the enormity of the overall failure. No riot can continue beyond a few hours without the active connivance of the local police and magistracy. The blood of hundreds of innocents are on the hands of the police and civil authorities of Gujarat, and by sharing in a conspiracy of silence, on the hands of the entire higher bureaucracy of the country.*

I have heard senior officials blame also the communalism, the alleged irrational sectarian hatred, of the police constabulary for their connivance in the violence. This too is a thin and disgraceful alibi. The same forces have been known to act with impartiality and courage when led by officers of professionalism and integrity. The failure is clearly of the leadership of the police and civil services, not of the subordinate men and women in khaki who are trained to obey their orders.

Where also, amidst this savagery, injustice, and human suffering was the famed 'civil society', the Gandhians, the development workers, the NGOs, the fabled spontaneous Gujarati philanthropy which was so much in evidence in the earthquake in Kutch and Ahmedabad? The newspapers reported that at the peak of the pogrom, the gates of

Sabarmati Asram were closed to protect its properties. It should instead have been the city's major sanctuary. There were some valiant and resplendent exceptions, but apart from them few Gandhian leaders, or NGO managers, staked their lives to halt the death-dealing throngs. It is one more shame that we as citizens of this country must carry on our already burdened backs that the camps for the Muslim riot victims in Ahmedabad and other parts of Gujarat were run almost exclusively by Muslim organizations. It was as though the monumental pain, loss, betrayal and injustice suffered by the Muslim people is the concern only of other Muslim people, and the rest of us have no share in the responsibility to assuage, to heal and rebuild. The state, which bears the primary responsibility to extend both protection and relief to its vulnerable citizens, was nowhere in evidence in any of the camps, to manage, organize the security, or even to provide the resources that are required to feed the tens of thousands of defenceless women, men and children huddled in these camps for safety.

The only passing moments of pride and hope that I experienced in those early desolate days in Gujarat were when I saw men like Mujid Ahmed and women like Roshan Bahen who served in these camps with tireless, dogged humanism amidst the ruins around them. In the Aman Chowk camp in Ahmedabad, women blessed the young band of volunteers who worked from four in the morning until after midnight to ensure that none of their children went without food or milk, or that their wounds remained untended. Their leader Mujid Ahmed is a graduate, his small chemical dyes factory has been burnt down, but he has had no time to worry about his own loss. Each day he had to find 1600 kilograms of foodgrain to feed some 5000 people who had taken shelter in the camp. The challenge was even greater for Roshan Bahen, almost 60, who wiped her eyes each time she heard the stories of horror by the residents in Juhapara camp. But she too had no time for the luxuries of grief or anger. She barely slept, as her volunteers, mainly working-class Muslim women and men from the humble tenements around the camp, provided temporary toilets, food and solace to the hundreds who had gathered in the grounds of a primary school to escape the ferocity of merciless mobs.

As I walked through the camps, I wondered what Gandhiji would have done in these dark hours. I recall the story of the Calcutta riots, when Gandhi was fasting for peace. A Hindu man came to him, to speak of his young son who had been killed by Muslim mobs, and of the plummetting depths of his anger and longing for revenge. And Gandhi is said to have replied: If you really wish to overcome your pain, find a young boy, just as young as your son, a Muslim boy whose parents have been killed by Hindu mobs. Bring up that boy like you would your own son, but bring him up with the Muslim faith to which he was born. Only then will you find that you can heal your pain, your anger, and your longing for retribution.

There are no voices like Gandhi's that we hear today. Only discourses on Newtonian physics, to justify vengeance on innocents. We need to find these voices within our own hearts, we need to believe enough in justice, love, tolerance.

There is much that the murdering mobs in Gujarat have robbed from me. One of them is a song I often sang with pride and conviction. The words of the song are:

Sare jahan se achha
Hindustan hamara…
*(Better than all the world,
is our India)
It is a song I will never be able to sing again.*

1

Borders: Living with Fear and Hate

In the later decades of India's struggle for freedom from British colonial rule, an immense groundswell of popular support and mass mobilization surged behind Mahatma Gandhi. A vast majority of Indians shared Gandhi's vision for the new India—a resolutely secular nation, with freedom and equal rights of citizenship for people of every faith, community, caste, class, colour and gender. There was also influential mass support for more radically egalitarian and democratic ideologies of the left and Dalit movements. However, leaders of the Muslim League fought for and secured an independent Islamic nation carved out from Muslim majority segments of India, convinced that people of diverse faiths cannot live together with peace and equality. Extremist Hindu organizations were also implacably opposed to Gandhi's humane and inclusive Hinduism and nationalism, and one reared among their ranks assassinated him just months after India became free.

The tolerant and pluralist secularism of modern India is rooted in millennia of the civilizational experience of India's populace, a civilization in which every major faith in the world found a home, was nurtured, and evolved, alongside a rich and challenging diversity of sceptical, rationalist, atheistic and agnostic beliefs. Indian secularism entails, therefore, not a denial of faith, but equal respect for *all* faiths—including the absence of faith—with all the symbols, philosophical trappings and ethical imperatives of these different systems of belief. In its modern incarnation of democratic secularism, it is overlaid with not just equal respect for all faiths, but also the guarantee for the practitioners of these diverse faiths of equal rights and protection under the secular law of the country. Secularism in India derives from an unbroken tapestry of the practice and teachings of tolerance and love, including those of the Buddha, Ashok, Akbar, Kabir, Nanak, the Sufi saints and Bhakti reformers, and Gandhi.

Two years after Gandhi fell to the bullets of his assassin, the Constitution of independent India—drafted by one of India's most revered leaders from a community traditionally subjected to the most savage caste discrimination, B.R. Ambedkar—further secured the secular, socialist and democratic foundations of the nation. This secular Constitution pledged equal freedoms and rights to all citizens regardless of their religion, gender, caste, ethnicity and language, including the freedom to not just follow but also propagate their own religion.

The struggle for freedom was never just a battle against colonial bondage, but also one for the India that would emerge when the British left Indian soil. It is significant that many of those who campaigned for the secular democratic idea of India, such as Gandhi and Maulana Azad, were devout practitioners of their respective religious faiths. On the other hand, foremost among those who fought for states constructed along religious lines, Jinnah—father of the Pakistani nation—was not a practising Muslim for most of his life, and Savarkar, founder of militant Hindu nationalism which he called Hindutva, was an avowed atheist. The battle, therefore, was never between the actual teachings of any religion. It was really about whether political mobilization and institutions should be based on identity and difference, or on acceptance of, respect for and even celebration of diversity.

Despite the solemn guarantees of the Constitution of free India and the proud and incandescent legacy of Gandhi and his non-violent movement—dimmed and shaken but by no means extinguished by the slaughter that accompanied Partition—pseudo-religious fascistic organizations continue to challenge the secular democratic vision for India. Their onslaughts have grown more militant since the 1980s, with a resurgence of their aggressive politics of difference and hate, and their propagation of a homogenized, combative, patriarchal and upper-caste version of the essentially pluralist majority Hindu faith. The most powerful symbol of this mobilization is the crumbling medieval mosque, the Babri Masjid, in Ayodhya, which they claim had been constructed after demolishing a temple built to commemorate the birthplace of Lord Ram. A massive mob assault on this Muslim place of worship resulted in its brutish demolition in 1992. As the highest courts of the country unconscionably prevaricate in their attempts to arbitrate the rival claims to the disputed site, extremist Hindu organizations continue to demand stridently that the site of the destroyed mosque be handed over for the construction of the Ram temple regardless of the decision of the courts, or independent historical and archaeological evidence. The movement to build a temple at the precise site of the mosque, is not about competing reverence for Ram or Allah, but an assault on the idea of secular democratic India itself.

The events leading up to the carnage in Gujarat in the spring of 2002 began with one of the innumerable mass campaigns that are periodically organized—more vigorously in the run-up to various elections—by the fascistic Hindutva organizations which collectively describe themselves as the Sangh Parivar. Led by the old men in khaki shorts who head the Rashtriya Sevak Sangh (RSS), these include the Vishwa Hindu Parishad (VHP), the lumpen youth formation called the Bajrang Dal, the Bharatiya Janata Party (BJP) and their student wing, the Akhil Bhartiya Vidyarthi Parishad.

A train-load of activists was returning to Gujarat from Ayodhya following one such campaign on 27 February 2002. At the railway station in the small town of Godhra, in Gujarat, a railway compartment of the Sabarmati Express went up in flames, resulting in the horrific death by burning alive of fifty-eight people, many of them women and children. It was widely and influentially propagated immediately by both the state government and Hindutva organizations that the incident was the result of merciless arson planned and executed by a terrorist mob of Muslim people who lived close to the railway station. This was used efficiently but recklessly as an instrument to dangerously ignite prejudice and hatred against the entire population of Muslim people living in Gujarat and indeed everywhere in India, and to justify their slaughter and rape and subsequent socio-economic boycott all across Gujarat. (However, later forensic investigation has led many human rights activists, legal and forensic experts to contest the official version of the source of the fire in the Sabarmati Express. Independent judicial authorities, notably the Justice Bannerjee Commission, rejected the idea of arson and concluded instead, on the basis of convincing forensic and circumstantial evidence, that the fire was most probably the result of an accident. Another judicial commission, headed by Justice Nanavati, appointed by the state government, on the other hand, upholds the government version of a terrorist conspiracy.)

Within hours of the burning of the train, cities, towns and villages across the state were convulsed by murders, arson, looting and rape, on a scale and brutality rarely seen in independent India, holding the entire Muslim community responsible for the alleged crime of setting the train on fire. Among the myriad aching images and voices that I have chronicled in this volume—and will carry in my heart throughout my life—are of young girls and women being gang-raped, often in the presence of other members of their families, and then being burned alive or bludgeoned to death. A young boy in a relief camp insisted on telling a visiting fact-finding team of women activists what 'rape' meant. 'It means making a woman naked, and setting her on fire.' A broken old man, insane with grief, who lost his entire family, shared with me the story of his life, wondering why he was still alive.

Through Gujarat and the unspeakable mass terror and savagery unleashed by organized bands of armed young men spurred by hate in the name of religion the country hurtled back into the trauma of Partition, which had left a million people dead and the nation dismembered. Through Gujarat, we relive the thousands of episodes of sectarian slaughter, and open or disguised pogroms against India's minorities, which have repeatedly wounded and disgraced the country with stunning constancy in these many years since we won our freedom. The events of 2002, and their aftermath of persisting hate and unmitigated fear even after so many years, bring to the fore not just a gruesome pogrom planned and executed with active and unrepentant state complicity, but a polity and society poisoned by the systematic manufacture of hatred, which has reduced people belonging to minority faiths to second-class citizens, truly to children of a lesser god.

Little has changed for the survivors of the Gujarat carnage of 2002, despite the passage of more than seven years and a major change of regime in New Delhi. A climate of fear and hostility, as well as economic and social boycott, still pervades many parts of Gujarat, and many tens of thousands of survivors continue to languish without hope, security, homes and livelihoods. The state government, triumphantly re-elected after the massacre both in 2002 and 2007, refuses to reach out with the resources and support to enable people devastated by the carnage to rebuild their lives. It also continues to subvert the judicial system in unprecedented ways to deny justice to the survivors. The widely shared assumption is that after the stunning electoral endorsement months after the carnage in the winter of 2002 and repeated emphatically five years later in 2007, 'normalcy', economic prosperity and peace were restored to the ravaged state. But my repeated journeys into Gujarat over these past years reveal the frightening face of this utterly counterfeit peace, based on a resigned social acceptance of settled fear, unequal compromises and the culture and practices of enforced second-class citizenship.

There are 'borders' within the state now. People have drawn lines between sections of each city and village in which one or the other community is amassed, and are afraid to cross these borders. They speak routinely today of the divide between 'their' ghettoes and 'our' (shining) city. Reports appeared in the local press of resolutions by sections of professionals like doctors and lawyers, as well as traders, to boycott Muslim clients in the days after the carnage. The services of thousands of Muslim employees were abruptly terminated in those dark times. Gujarati middle-class men and women boast of their refusal to engage even a rickshaw with a Muslim driver.

People from the minorities today find it nearly impossible to rent houses in segments of the city outside their own ghettoes. Even opening a bank account is difficult if one carries a Muslim name. Mothers advise their sons to shave their beards, and outside their ghettoes auto rickshaws and hotels owned by Muslims almost never display symbols that reveal Islamic identities. National newspapers published reports that Muslims altered their names when admitting themselves in hospitals or travelling in trains, because they feared so desperately for their safety. However, inhabitants of the shining cities claim that nothing changed for them after the 2002 violence except that they take new roads to work—roads that by-pass the 'dangerous' Muslim ghettoes, roads that Muslim rickshaw pullers do not want to ply on for they are built over their razed shrines.

There are many villages in Gujarat today that exult in having 'cleansed' themselves of their erstwhile Muslim residents. There are gaily painted boards at the entrance of some of these villages: 'Welcome to this Hindu village in the Hindu Rashtra of Gujarat'. These hoardings, erected by the VHP, had begun to appear as early as 1998 in many parts of Gujarat in the mounting campaign of militant Hindutva, but they have proliferated since 2002. The victims of these acts of social 'cleansing' are struggling to live with a government and neighbours that deny their losses and displacement. It is estimated that more than half of the affected people are still unable to return to the soil of their ancestors, and indeed today despair of ever returning to their homes. There are still others who choose not to return to the land of their birth. Instead, they huddle together in crowded Muslim ghettoes, or live in small tenements in unrecognised relief colonies, without minimal public services, struggling to find work and grappling with their painful memories, all the while desperately searching for the safety of numbers.

Those who have negotiated their return to their original villages are wrestling with economic boycott and social marginalization in segregated colonies. Living with economic boycott is hard enough, but much harder is to walk down the village street each day when no one greets you, no one calls you to a wedding. There are villages where, each morning, women gather, collect cowdung and throw it in the village kabristan. The survivors know they have nowhere else to go. They suffer crippling social and economic embargoes and humiliating compromises as the price of returning to their homes to gather the shattered pieces of their lives. They are barred from pursuing legal justice, or giving evidence against their tormentors to the police or courts, irrespective of the crimes committed against them. They are forced to live in separate settlements, denied employment and trade, and told that the call of the azaan should under no circumstances resound in the village. The acceptance of these conditions amounts to abject social surrender by an entire minority community, a forced consent to live as second-class citizens. The fact that thousands are accepting these terms, and that there is little public resistance or outrage in Gujarat and elsewhere against this denial of basic citizenship, makes the aftermath of 2002 even more chilling, with congealed covert violence embedded in transformed social relations.

Authentic peace can be founded ultimately only on justice, trust and dignity. In the wake of blood-drenched betrayal and mass brutality, the construction of an enduring peace requires both the healing of remorse and compassion and the demonstration of justice done. Unfortunately, neither of these are evident anywhere in the seven years after the carnage of 2002 in this troubled state.

2

To Love Again?
Paths to Reconciliation

Of the many failures that characterize the polity and society in contemporary Gujarat, probably the most dangerous is the unprecedented extent of the arrest and collapse of processes of authentic reconciliation. The state remains openly hostile to a segment of citizens only because they belong to a different faith. The speeches of senior elected public leaders, especially Chief Minister Narendra Modi, are peppered with raucous and openly prejudiced sectarian taunts. They continually cast aspersions on the patriotism of Muslim citizens, parody their supposedly pervasive practices of polygamy and breeding large families, decry the alleged slaughter of cows, and claim their wide sympathies with terrorist violence. Muslim youths are arrested randomly on charges of terrorism, and their deaths in so-called 'encounters' or extra-judicial killings are explained away by state authorities often without a shred of any credible evidence of their terrorist activities. Their Muslim identity is accepted as reason enough to believe that they must have been terrorists, and 'terrorists' do not deserve the protection of law. People of diverse faiths live side by side or in segregated ghettoes but in an uneasy, warped, brittle truce, without genuine trust and normal social and economic interaction.

There are few organized social and political spaces—official or non-official—in Gujarat today for fostering forgiveness and compassion. There is instead a frightening communal chasm, accepted and even actively encouraged by the powerful political, administrative, business and media establishments. This engineered divide is growing exponentially between people of different religious persuasions. An ominous subtext characterizes re-engineered social relations: Gujarat continues to be a society bitterly and, some now grimly fear, permanently divided.

❧

After the communal bloodbath that accompanied the vivisection of the country as it seized its independence, there have been thousands of riots, episodes of mass clashes between people of Hindu and Muslim faith, and pogroms, resulting in the loss, according to one painstaking estimate, of at least 25,628 lives (including 1005 in police firings).[1] Yet, despite this recurring communal bloodletting, there has been no systematic structured official (or even significant non-official) process of 'truth and reconciliation' to help perpetrators and survivors of hate violence come together; acknowledge their crimes and failings, their hate and fear, their grievances and suspicions; to seek and offer forgiveness, restore trust and goodwill; and ultimately bring closure and eventual healing. Given the enormity of contemporary threats posed by a deliberately fostered communal divide and violence to the very survival of secular democracy in India, fuelled further by the manufactured global 'war on terror', it is imperative that systematic, sustained processes of reconciliation and justice in communal relations between people of diverse faiths and ethnicities in India are established.

Part of the problem is that the threats and grave peril of on-going communal violence and pervasive subversion of justice to minorities are not sufficiently acknowledged by the state, political parties and formal civil society organizations. Even as relations between communities deteriorate dangerously, and states become openly partisan on communal lines and soft on organizations that are committed to destroy the secular democratic foundations of the nation state, many in the country continue to live in denial. Secondly, much of the violence and injustice is not overt; it rages unseen in the hearts and minds of people. We respond, however inadequately, only when the violence actually spills on to the streets, when our pavements are soaked in human blood, when the bodies of girls and women are violated, and when the smoke of burnt homes and shops rises to the skies, leaving behind the rubble of vandalized hopes and dreams. Thirdly, governments, political parties and social organizations are today most frequently equivocal, unsteady and reluctant in dealing with the intensely sensitive and potentially divisive issues raised by communalism.

In the absence of structured modes of facilitating reconciliation for survivors of the cataclysmic Partition violence of 1947, some may argue that adequate closure for families that experienced the agony and permanent separation from and the irreparable loss of their loved ones and homeland. My own parents and their extended families lost their homes amidst hate, slaughter and arson in a region of the country that became a part of Pakistan in 1947, and their grief remains dormant more than sixty years later, just below the surface. Perhaps we needed much earlier to bring together people who lived with the violence from both sides of the border, to share truth, discover their common burdens of suffering and privation, and thereby find the spaces for individual and collective forgiveness.

However, the Indian people have arguably had more experience than most of living with diversity, therefore even without organized processes of reconciliation, there are usually natural, spontaneous processes of reaching out and healing that follow bouts of sectarian violence.[2] In other communal conflagrations that I have witnessed and handled in small district towns as a district administrator, I have observed individual and collective acts of spontaneous goodwill and compassion reach out from each community within days of such mass upheavals. There are widespread expressions of remorse and grief at the loss suffered by the other community, and of kindness, through which processes of social and personal healing set in.

By contrast, the defining feature of Gujarat after the 2002 massacre is the determined absence of remorse in both the state and many segments of the people. The conspicuous absence of social and political processes of reconciliation, and the resultant divide and distrust between the estranged communities heightens this lack of compassion. Unsurprisingly, almost seven years later, what is most scarce in the parched earth of allegedly vibrant Gujarat is reconciliation and empathy. The natural, spontaneous human and social responses of compassion are deliberately contained by social stratagems of manufactured hate and the politics of divide. A profoundly new understanding of the self is being forged through fear and revulsion of the demonised 'other'. The agony of Gujarat—its blood-drenched humanity soaked in ideologies of hatred and divide—has brought the people of our vast and ancient land to a defining crossroads.

Reconciliation is not a new instrument that the world has recently fashioned in our efforts to overcome historical conflicts and build enduring peace among divided and embattled mortals. On the contrary, warring and bitterly estranged peoples have from time to time wearied of battles and hate, of destruction and fear, buried their weapons and collectively sought or rediscovered ways of living together with peace, faith and goodwill. In lay terms, reconciliation is the process by which mutual dialogue, understanding, trust and amity are restored between members of different racial, ethnic, religious, social or economic groups who have been divided by mass violence, organized campaigns of hate or prolonged oppression. This restoration aspires to achieve levels of shared living and social relations that at least match those that existed before the conflict began, or to even higher levels that are mutually considered more acceptably just and egalitarian, and ultimately a genuine meeting of hearts and minds.

Reconciliation has a history of varied meanings in official, legal and political discourses. For the state and dominant groups, ideas of collective and institutionalized reconciliation—facilitated by officials and political leaders and, sometimes, by social workers—have often been used to coerce the oppressed into being 'reconciled' to existing iniquitous notions of social order. Family courts are also a striking example in which survivors of domestic violence are encouraged to 'reconcile' to their secondary situation in the family, without challenging the injustice of patriarchy or the violence of unequal partnerships. An ethical value is placed on women to accept oppressed realities for the 'peace' of the home. This is not very different from the counterfeit 'reconciliation'—in truth, submission—which is frequently imposed on powerless minorities. This monograph is concerned with searching for paths to egalitarian and just reconciliation, and will attempt to shift focus to the discourse of survivors, attempting to understand even a little of what authentic reconciliation means to them.

Although reconciliation is a timeless process, the word itself has only recently entered, and since then significantly illuminated, the literature of peace-building and conflict resolution. The idea has gained in the popular global imagination especially after the influential Truth and Reconciliation Commission of post-apartheid South Africa was established in 1995, as a novel way for a virulently divided and antagonistic nation to heal itself though truth telling. Peace-building itself became a popular concept after the United Nations secretary-general Boutros Boutros-Ghali spoke of it in his 'Agenda for Peace' in 1992.

Efforts for reconciliation are spurred by the understanding that stable peace can only occur when the issues that led to the conflict in the first place are addressed to the satisfaction of all. 'Without reconciliation, the best one can normally hope for is the kind of temporary truce'.[3] In the absence of reconciliation hate is retained and nurtured, with stereotypes, myths, selective memory and lies about the demonised 'other', and passed on as a dubious legacy from one generation to the next. In recent times, memory has been abused, for instance, to 'fuel the fires of hatred' in Northern Ireland, and in the completely varied recollections of their common history by Albanians and Serbs in Kosovo, and Muslims and Serbs in Bosnia.[4] This collective distorted memory of falsehoods and deliberate half-truths has also been used globally to create a climate of distrust against people of the Muslim faith in the so-called global war on terror.

Speaking to an audience on the need for reclaiming and defending a secular India, in Ludhiana, I recall being confronted by an elderly man in the audience who wept painfully, 'My family was uprooted from Pakistan in 1947, and it lost many lives at the hands of Muslims. What can I tell my children? How do you expect me to tell them to forgive and forget?' I told him that my own family belonged to

Rawalpindi and had suffered in similar ways. 'But why should Muslim men, women and children today deserve hatred, and even worse retribution, for crimes that other Muslims may have committed decades ago? And more importantly, why is our memory so selective? If you must recall to your children the crimes suffered by Hindus and Sikhs during Partition, should you not recount to them also the fact that their Hindu and Sikh ancestors committed exactly the same unspeakable atrocities against Muslims on this side of the border?'

The falsehoods and half-truths of memory rob the 'other' of not just equal citizenship, but even elementary humanity. In all communal squalls, the bodies of women are specially targeted. Women's bodies are refashioned as the property of the hated 'other' and as symbols of their honour, therefore attacks on these aim to humiliate the men who 'own' them and help break their spirit. Imposed consent for silence as forms of spurious reconciliation are likely to muffle the unhealed agony of women survivors most of all. In Gujarat in 2002, we witnessed the recurrent use of women's bodies as battlefields in the carnage of hate, and the extraordinary support of many women of the majority Hindu community for these acts of mass sexual violence. These women stopped seeing Muslim women in their own likeness, and allowed the politics of hate to distort their perception and regard Muslim women as deserving of the same violence which, if targeted towards themselves, would have humiliated and crushed them.

It is hard for me as a man to even speculate what reconciliation means to women who survived rape. And even more so to those who continue to face the torments of their rapists living unpunished within their own communities. Feminist observers perceive a change in 'rape cultures' in Gujarat following the brutally gendered violence of 2002, even in relation to Hindu women, and the increased trafficking of women and girls in marriage and on the sex market.[5] In the painful stoic or muffled silences of the survivors, the questions still shout to be heard about whether there is an impossibility of reconciliation for survivors of rape, especially when the rapists and those who instigated them walk free. Who can speak to them of finding spaces in their hearts for forgiveness, and who indeed should? Do such paths exist at all for the women who carry burdens of the pain and humiliation such as of 2002? If such paths exist, they must, I believe, traverse also the daunting treacherous journey of justice.

Ideas of reconciliation and forgiveness—as well as justice—are intrinsic in varied but related ways to virtually every major strand of diverse religious and secular convictions that have impinged through the centuries on the consciousness of the Indian people. It is inspiring to recall even today that more than sixty years ago, in an inconsolable country grieving bitterly for a million lives extinguished by Partition, homes and homelands lost forever and a country dismembered by the divisive politics of hate, Gandhi's last battle before his assassination in January 1948 was for the rights of the Muslim people. Not just those who had chosen secular democratic India as their home, but also those who had opted for the religious state of Pakistan. The conviction that drove him all through his life was that 'There is no way to peace. Peace is the way.' He spoke of peace as 'a heavy downpour of rain which drenches the soil to fullness, likewise only a profuse shower of love overcomes hatred'. His comments on forgiving and forgetting are illuminating: 'To forgive is not to forget. The merit lies in loving in spite of the vivid knowledge that the one that must be loved is not a friend. There is no merit in loving an enemy when you forget him for a friend.'

Reconciliation is understood as not stopping at finding solutions to objective problems that people perceive as causing conflict; it is necessarily a voluntary process undertaken by people involved in historical conflicts to come to terms with memories of an anguished past, and to build together a resolve to move forward to a peaceful future. Though it cannot be imposed externally, external actors such as the state can certainly help facilitate, support and encourage the process. Shriver persuasively argues that 'precisely because it attends at once to moral truth, history, and the human benefits that flow from the conquest of enmity, reconciliation is a word for a multidimensional process that is eminently political'.

The imperatives for reconciliation globally and historically may derive from both religious and secular sources.[6] Several discussions around reconciliation are drawn from religious teachings, such as those related to righteousness, religious duty, confession, repentance and atonement. Others find inspiration in human rights, stressing equality before law, equal citizenship and equal protection by law, religious and cultural rights of minorities and deterrence of recurrence by fair application of law to all citizens. There are also secular appeals and approaches to reconciliation that do not derive only from the legal system, but resort to ethical beliefs in the essential goodness and ultimate 'reclaim-ability' of every human being, equal worth of all people, and the intrinsic values of tolerance, democracy and non-violence.

The ultimate objective of reconciliation is to re-establish the parameters of safe and secure co-existence between estranged and conflicting communities. At a minimal level, it can amount only to a compact to live together under sufferance, without goodwill or trust or intercourse, only the mutual self-interested resolve to abjure violence. I recall the words of a peace-activist friend, who has devoted the best years of his life to strengthen Hindu–Muslim unity in India, said in a moment of dark despair. 'I have given up hoping that Hindus and Muslims will love each other. Today for me it is enough that they do not kill one another.' Such minimalist reconciliation does not eliminate conflict, but only reduces the resort to individual or collective violations of body and property as the means to resolve this. Reconciliation is deepened when it travels well beyond such a resolve to continue to hate but not destroy, to one that positively builds trust, confidence and eventually empathy between previously embroiled people.[7]

c⌒ɔ

Drawing on a large part of the literature around reconciliation, Hamber and Kelly (2004) have developed a thoughtful, comprehensive and influential list of the activities they consider essential to any process of reconciliation. They regard reconciliation as a 'process of addressing conflictual and fractured relationships' which involves developing a shared vision of an interdependent, just, equitable, open and diverse society. It includes acknowledging the hurt, loss, truth and suffering of the past, providing mechanisms that offer justice, healing, restitution or reparation, and restoration. The next step is building positive relationships while addressing issues of trust, prejudice, and intolerance, thereby accepting commonalities and differences, and embracing and engaging with those who are different from us. Reconciliation should result in significant cultural and attitudinal changes in how people relate to, and their behaviour towards, one another. The culture of suspicion, fear, mistrust and violence is broken down, and opportunities and space created in which people can hear and be heard. A culture of respect for human rights and human difference is developed creating a context where each citizen becomes an active participant in society and feels a sense of belonging. According to Hamber and Kelly, reconciliation moves towards an outcome in which social, economic and political structures that gave rise to the conflict and estrangement are identified, reconstructed or addressed, and transformed.

I propose that any authentic process of reconciliation requires at least four mandatory components: acknowledgement; remorse; reparation; and justice. I am not suggesting that these elements must be accomplished chronologically in the order that I have listed them or indeed any other order, or that this is an exhaustive list. Instead, I maintain that these add up more to a set of values, political and ethical principles and pathways to restore egalitarian social intercourse. I have derived these as essential components of reconciliation from the specific context of my engagement with Gujarat after 2002, and recognize that the imperatives may vary in diverse political and social contexts with different histories of pain and loss.

The first of these elements, acknowledgement, involves public acceptance—not just by the perpetrators and the state authorities, but also by the people and organizations who supported the violence or were silent or indifferent as it unfolded—that violence and discrimination did take place, causing unconscionable pain and suffering to those who were targeted.

The second, remorse, is a public expression of collective sincere contrition for the hate, violence, injustice and suffering that transpired. In Hindi, it is called 'paschataap'.

Reparation—the third component—entails providing adequate and timely assistance to enable victim survivors to fashion shelters, livelihoods, common resources and cultural environments that are at least comparable to (and, I believe, better than) what they had prior to the conflict. This is in conformity with established principles of international law, under which restitution involves 're-establishment of the situation which existed before the wrongful act was committed'.[8] There can be no compensation for the loss of loved ones, homes and valued ways of life; reparation should still address, with humility and sensitivity, these losses to the extent that is humanly possible. For this, not just the impersonal state but also the perpetrators and the wrong-doers should be actively mobilized in the process of rebuilding. In the aftermath of the Gujarat 2002 massacre, some Hindu villagers in the region surrounding Godhra, the epicentre of the upheaval, voluntarily contributed to rebuilding the destroyed homes of their Muslim neighbours, an act that was intensely healing for the battered survivors.

The final component, justice, involves primarily legal justice, that is the equal application and protection of the law of the land by institutions of the state. It also includes accountability of the legal system of public officials who are charged with preventing and controlling communal violence, reparation and restoring peace. Ultimately, justice involves the establishment of a sustainable environment of harmony and amity based on legal and social principles, guarantees of non-repetition, freedom from fear and distrust between communities, and strengthening of social, economic and cultural bonds between them.

It is only when the crimes of the past are acknowledged, and atonement made with public expressions of genuine remorse, when the state, the perpetrator and survivor join hands to rebuild broken lives, and when justice is done and seen to have been done, is it possible for those who suffer to forgive, to heal, to trust and possibly to even love again.

&

It is often suggested that there is a self-evident conflict or disconnect, some would suggest even a contradiction, between the goals of formal justice and reconciliation. In the aftermath of Gujarat 2002, there are many who argue that the efforts of human rights groups such as the one I am engaged with, which strive to secure justice for the survivors, are actually blocking efforts at understanding, or the spaces for forgiveness. Such enterprises are seen to be akin to scraping the scab off old wounds and not letting them heal naturally: they are seen as not letting the survivors forget their suffering. Those opposed to such efforts dispute: 'What is achieved by reviving memories of what is done and over with? We should let the people affected by the admittedly unfortunate mass violence move on, without being constantly pulled into the quicksand of a painful past.'

It is significant that such suggestions are rarely made by those affected by the violence themselves, or those who suffer indirectly from the continuing injustice in Gujarat. They come mostly from people of the majority community who have not suffered the torment of the survivors of the carnage, who do not live with persisting insecurity and contested citizenship rights, or indeed with the harrowing impact of a drift into a re-engineered fascistic majoritarian social and political order. There are some among the affected communities in Gujarat— usually traders or better-off victims, and more men than women—who choose not to fight for legal justice. They do so not because they do not value justice, but as a practical act of individual survival in a climate of persisting hate and fear.

However, there was one authentic and painful call that did emerge from the victim survivor community for unilateral forgiveness by the Muslims for the crimes of 2002. In a signed article that appeared on-line nearly six years after the carnage, J.S. Bandukwala, a retired professor of physics from M.S. University in Vadodara, whose house was attacked twice and vandalized, speaks of his yearning for the 'healing touch of a Mahatma Gandhi' to bridge the divide between Hindus and Muslims.[9] He is himself convinced, as I have also argued, that reconciliation requires leaders of the aggressor Hindu community to express genuine remorse and for the victim Muslim community to forgive. Over six years, although he 'repeatedly urged Gujarati Hindu religious leaders, intellectuals and businessmen to come forward and apologize for the events of 2002 so that the process of uniting both communities can begin', by and large 'the response has been just stark silence'. He observes with great sorrow: 'We have begged religious figures to recognize that these rapes and murders were done in the name of Ram, and therefore as Ram bhakts they should condemn such monstrous acts. Sadly, there has been no public response from them, even after the perpetrators have openly gloated about their despicable acts. What is the point of preaching about God, ahimsa and vegetarianism, including a periodic demand for ban on the sale of eggs, when we remain silent about slashing pregnant women?'

Bandukwala despairs now of Hindu leaders ever regretting the crimes of 2002, and finds them instead celebrating the assaults. He grapples with the heart-breaking reality of deadlocked relations between the communities, and concludes that there is no way out except for the Muslim community to forgive unilaterally. He is convinced that 'such forgiveness by victims conforms to the highest traditions of Islam. It enriches the victim, rescues the aggressor and pleases Allah immensely. Islam teaches that ultimate justice can only come from Allah. Those who carried out these dastardly acts will have to answer their Creator. Political pressure or judicial manipulation will not work with the Divine.' Inspired by the teachings of the Koran, Bandukwala quotes (passage 41, 34): 'Good and evil cannot be equal. Repel evil with one which is better; then he between whom and you there was hatred will become your friend.'

Though he expresses gratitude to civil rights group 'for their fight on our behalf under the most adverse circumstances', Bandukwala feels that the Muslims of Gujarat cannot live indefinitely on what he sees as pity and victimhood. 'It hurts our self-respect and dignity. We have to move beyond the pain and suffering of 2002. Our energies must be channelled into quality education, business and social reform within the parameters of Islam ... Forgiveness will release Muslims from the trauma of the past. It may also touch the conscience of Hindus, since the crimes were committed by a few fanatics in the name of Ram. Most important, it may give Gujarat a chance to close the tragic chapter of 2002 and move on with confidence, into the future.'

There is a rare grace, dignity and magnanimity in Bandukwala's plea for unilateral forgiveness. Nevertheless, it is driven by despair at the refusal of leaders of the Hindu community to seek forgiveness, and unwillingness to live further with a sense of persecution. True healing cannot come from such a gesture of great dignity but hopelessness. There is no short-cut to a genuine meeting of hearts, except to persist with finding ways for truth, remorse, reparation and justice to emerge and pave the way for rebuilding not just lives but also hope and trust.

I am convinced that the decision to close the past without looking back must not be imposed on the people who live not only with the memories of the trauma of unspeakable loss and violence, but the daily realities of continued persecution, fear and hate. The survivors of Gujarat should not feel coerced into a spurious amnesia, imposed on them by those who did not suffer and by their absence of remorse and compassion.

It is only when the survivors are able to deal voluntarily with this painful past, ably assisted by society and the state, that they will be able to look to the future with optimism and confidence. Traditions like the annual ritualized mourning of Moharram or the commemoration of the Holocaust in museums acknowledge the importance of remembering, even while forgiving and letting go. Only when there is remorse and healing, is it possible for the populace to 'move on'. Else, as philosopher Santayana wisely prophesied, 'those who cannot remember the past are condemned to repeat it'. We have repeated the history of communal violence and pogroms too many times in India to risk further repetition through forgetting the great unhealed wounds of our recent history.

Imposed Forgiveness?
Learning from South Africa

Recently, on my first visit to South Africa, I was awestruck by accounts of the justly celebrated Truth and Reconciliation Commission of South Africa, constituted after the political end of apartheid. The commission has inspired at least a score of other such bodies in other countries which have attempted to assist their people to deal with a history of strife.[1] A review of the experiences of twenty such commissions found that though official investigations into state atrocities and terror have helped the survivors move ahead, they are poignantly torn between the need to remember and also to forget.[2]

I wondered what lessons could be learnt from the experience of the Truth and Reconciliation Commission to bridge the frightening communal chasm that is growing between people of different faiths in India. The urgency of this quest, as I have observed earlier, was that in sectarian strife in the past, including the tumultuous Partition of 1947, we tended to rely on spontaneous social processes of healing and bringing together estranged communities. But in Gujarat, we face an unprecedented situation of a persisting and smouldering breach and distrust, a government that remains openly hostile to a segment of its citizens based on their faith, and the virtual collapse of the social processes of reconciliation.

The South African Truth and Reconciliation Commission assured legal amnesty to all perpetrators of atrocities as long as they admitted their crimes before the commission in the glare of a watchful media. It was argued in defence of the South African commission that this was a major advance from earlier such bodies elsewhere, which negotiated amnesty behind closed doors, and behind the backs of the victims of these mass hate crimes. However, the truth is that even in South Africa this decision was hastily imposed from 'above', without adequate information and debate, let alone the democratic consent of millions of Black people who had lived with the indignities, injustice and terror of apartheid, even though the decision impacted how they dealt with their past and their futures. Hugo van der Merwe, a South African scholar, says that the ANC leadership at that time believed that 'for local dynamics to change, national intervention must first take place. This will then filter down, or create the conditions [and incentives] within which local actors can pursue reconciliation processes'.[3]

Desmond Tutu specifically rejects what he describes as the 'Nuremburg trial paradigm', suggesting that the victims (or human rights defenders) should not individually or collectively pursue legal charges against their persecutors, nor should the state authorities 'run the gauntlet of the normal judicial process' to bring them to trial and eventual punishment.[4] He offers some practical arguments, primarily that without this agreement, the apartheid leadership would not have acquiesced to a negotiated settlement, and the judicial system would have continued to be biased against the victims.

There can be both convincing rationales and debates about the compromises that are entered into by political leaderships in historically difficult moments of transition. I can understand (but not necessarily agree) if Tutu and Mandela defend the decision of assured amnesty for truth-tellers who committed unspeakable crimes of apartheid as the only one that was politically feasible at that moment in South African history, if they admit even the possibility that the decision may have been politically appropriate but at the same time *ethically* flawed. But my problem is with Tutu's *ethical* (and not political) arguments in defence of this amnesty, because these are intended to state moral principles that have much more universal application: briefly that even legally determined and imposed punishment is retribution, which in turn is vengeance, and therefore it is ethically wrong.

Using Nozick's (1981) description of retributive punishment meted out through the legal system as 'punishment inflicted as deserved for a past wrong', Crocker persuasively proposes many ways in which retribution is *not* revenge.[5] Retribution is given for a violation that is collectively accepted as wrong; it is constrained and establishes limits to the punishment that can be meted out to the wrong-doer; it is principled and takes no personal satisfaction from the suffering of the person who is punished. Most importantly, in our context of communal riots, it rejects the doctrine of collective guilt—that mere membership of an opposing group justifies revenge. I will argue that ethnic conflicts in India are mainly in the nature of disguised pogroms or genocides, in which there *are* clear victims and perpetrators, primarily the state and organizations that are dedicated to the manufacture of hatred and the instigation and planning of the sectarian violence. In these circumstances, retributive justice, by challenging impunity, negating counterfeit hierarchies of suffering between communities and re-establishing equality before the law between people of disjoined communities, necessarily paves the way for eventual restorative justice.

The dangers of 'reconciliation' imposed on unequal contenders are further highlighted by Sumanta Banerjee who asks the difficult question—Was the advance assurance of amnesty for apartheid crimes only a fig-leaf to disguise the surrender imposed on the victims to forgo their rights to secure justice from their powerful oppressors?[6] Banerjee points out the paradox that while Winnie Mandela, wife of legendary ANC leader Nelson Mandela, was imprisoned on charges of fraud and theft during the apartheid regime, the white racists got away even with the killing of the famous South African radical leader Steven Biko. Biko's murderers, when brought before the commission, confessed their crimes in gory detail. But when Biko's family tried to institute a case against them, they were denied because the perpetrators were granted amnesty by the commission for admitting their guilt. He describes this bitterly as a 'novel method indeed to bring about reconciliation between the oppressor and the oppressed—at the cost of justice'. Sumanta Banerjee's even more trenchant criticism is that neither the apartheid regime nor the vast socio-economic disparities were put to trial in the quest for truth. As a result, the leaders of the apartheid regime were never held accountable, and '95 percent of the economy [continues to be] controlled by the same white settlers who created apartheid'. Data also show that 47.8 per cent of black people were unemployed in 2003 compared to only 9.9 per cent of whites.[7] Thus, the victims of apartheid were denied the right to bring their oppressors to legal justice by the democratic leadership of new South Africa.

Truth-telling was the only explicit requirement of the Truth and Reconciliation Commission for qualifying for amnesty; no expression of remorse was deemed necessary. I have argued earlier that for reconciliation to be authentic, it requires at least four components: acknowledgement, remorse, reparation and justice. The Truth and Reconciliation Commission most powerfully assured only one of these components—acknowledgement—and to some extent it organized reparation for some of the victims. Although it did not require remorse, Desmond Tutu, who chaired the commission, and Fazel Randera, one of the commissioners whom I met in Johannesburg, affirmed that a great deal of genuine regret was spontaneously forthcoming from those who testified to often chilling crimes before the commission. But the assurance of amnesty traded away—and many like me believe very cheaply—the requirements of legal justice, although others may persuasively argue that the larger ends of restorative justice were indeed achieved. I observed strong disagreement and dissatisfaction among many black South Africans with Mandela's call for collective forgiveness for the brutal crimes of the recent past. Forgiveness, to be authentic and genuinely healing, must be the voluntary, informed and empowered choice of the survivors. It cannot—*must not*—be forced on them. 'Legal forgetting' which is politically imposed antagonizes the survivor and does not bring about any real closure for the individual, nor for the divided societies which parties the whole.[8] To free offenders from the legal consequences of their actions amounts to trading away justice in return for a kind of unequal peace. The post-Second-World-war amnesty laws passed in France and Holland for people who had collaborated with the Germans met with similar dissatisfaction and disagreement, as did those in many Latin American countries in the 1980s.[9]

There can be little doubt that the statesmanship and magnanimity of the ANC leadership, embodied in Nelson Mandela, and unique humanitarian enterprises like the Truth and Reconciliation Commission, helped avert bloodletting of the kind that literally tore the Indian nation apart in 1947 (and subsequently the Pakistani nation in 1971). This in itself is an enormous historic achievement. The Truth and

Reconciliation Commission hearings also helped the nation, and particularly its black populations, confront and, to some degree, come to terms with the savage oppression of the nightmarish apartheid decades. In the cathartic hearings of the commission, black survivors frequently displayed extraordinary humanity in forgiving their tormentors. As Tutu repeatedly affirms, there is indeed no future without forgiveness.

However, in my short stay in South Africa, I repeatedly encountered a country that remains deeply fractured on racial and overlapping class lines, as well as gender; between African, coloured, Indian and white, men and women. There are further divisions, of ethnic groups within the Blacks, the Indians, the Afrikaaner and the white people. The colour of one's skin remains the overwhelming defining feature of one's identify, opportunities and social relations in South Africa, although the last decade has seen the emergence of a small but growing Black middle class seeking to escape the centuries-old confines of race. The incredibly luxurious suburbs are still populated almost exclusively by white people, whereas in the crowded and deprived shanties, it is rare to encounter anyone other than black men, women and children. And within each and between each of these are chilling narratives of rape and sexual violence.

The Truth and Reconciliation Commission should not have been a one-off event. A great deal more needed to be done to make the commission a sustained process, especially for dialogue and understanding, bringing together people from across various racial and class divides on an egalitarian platform.

Fazel Randera said to me, 'I do believe that building on the Truth and Reconciliation Commission process of staring truth in the eye and actively negotiating the society we wish to build, will help overcome many of the problems that not only we face but the world faces. Even class will eventually be peacefully negotiated away.' I am not persuaded. Inequality, racism, patriarchy and injustice will have to be fought constantly by people's resolute democratic (and, I am convinced, non-violent) struggles and state action. There are no painless short-cuts to equality, equity or justice. Not even truth, forgiveness and mercy, even though I deeply believe in all of these.

Acknowledgement and some reparation, without remorse and justice, are not enough for reconciliation to occur. Is legal justice intrinsically just retributive or is it equally or even more importantly an assertion of equal citizenship rights, is a question that we repeatedly return to in this book. To my mind, reconciliation is necessarily an egalitarian process, and cannot be founded on a surrender of one's rights, dignity and aspirations from a position of weakness. True forgiveness requires a prior establishment of a situation of sufficient equality of power to enable persons who suffered *not* to forgive if they so choose, and for their choice to have consequences on those whom they elect not to forgive. For this reason, I believe that justice and remorse are both intrinsic to an authentic and enduring process of reconciliation.

I left South Africa after an admittedly short visit with a number of questions. Has the Truth and Reconciliation Commission really healed wounds? Has it joined hearts across the racial divide? Have the survivors of apartheid really forgiven and moved on, especially black populations and women? I acknowledge that it is unfair to expect that the ravages of centuries of colonial rule and fifty years of legalized racism can disappear with one commission and a decade and a half of democracy. Though it did prevent untold bloodshed and sectarian slaughter, staggering economic and racial inequality persists. South Africa remains hopelessly divided on racial lines, with the privileges or deprivations of class mostly reinforcing those of race and gender. Oppression and injustice, not only of the past but also the present, are engines of dangerous anger among the youth, reflected in a murky sub-culture of brutalized street violence and crime.

I strongly believe that official or non-official efforts for reconciliation should never be even a well-intentioned apology for impunity for crimes, especially by state authorities, and others who enjoy positions of power. Legal accountability for atrocities and crimes paves the way for genuine reconciliation, although it does not guarantee the same. As Tina Rosenberg writes, 'If the victims in a society do not feel that their suffering has been acknowledged, then they . . . are not ready to put the past behind them. If they know that the horrible crimes carried out in secret will always remain buried . . . then they are not ready for reconciliation.'[10]

The context of the South African Truth and Reconciliation Commission, and of any similar process that we may choose to apply in Gujarat between the bitterly estranged Hindu and Muslim communities, is vastly different from Gujarat's in several ways. The Truth and Reconciliation Commission was initiated *after* the political battle against apartheid was won. In Gujarat, we are embroiled in a situation in which communal ideologies remain triumphant and in power in the state, and indeed in many parts of the country. In fact, a large sprinkling of members of centrist and even left political formations is clandestinely, and sometimes even openly, sympathetic to communal ideologies.

India has a long history of communal violence that leaves behind survivors seeking justice. Every major outbreak of communal violence, including the Gujarat carnage of 2002, is followed by the establishment of judicial commissions of enquiries, headed by sitting or retired judges of the high courts or the Supreme Court.[11] These commissions are effectively also truth commissions, although they are not so designated and do not allow the participation of the diverse segments of society, a feature that gave the South African Truth and Reconciliation Commission so much credibility and attention. These commissions enjoy the support of the rule of law and the Constitution. But, unlike other such bodies, judicial commissions are more spaces for victims to appear before and testify and give evidence against the crimes that they have suffered, and for state and state agents to defend their actions, rather than for the perpetrators of mass crimes to admit to their transgressions. Although many judicial commissions have, indeed with integrity, courage and fairness, uncovered painful and uncomfortable truths, which have exposed the crimes of not just private individuals but also state authorities and sectarian organizations that often enjoy the tacit support and encouragement of the state, none of those named by the commission have been adequately punished for their crimes. Both the Shrikrishna Report on the Mumbai riots of 1993-94 and the Nanavati Commission investigating the 1984 anti-Sikh riots in Delhi met with the same inaction.

If a people's truth and reconciliation commission were to be instituted in Gujarat, it would probably carry far more moral authority than the judicial commission (headed by retired judges Justice Nanavati and the late Justice Shah) that was instituted by the same state government which is widely seen as complicit in the crimes of 2002 and devoid of even the pretensions of secular convictions.

But even a non-official people's truth and reconciliation commission would not alter the reality of people who survived the carnage only to live in the shadow of fear, unable to return to their homes, facing economic and social boycott in the rare instances where they have indeed returned. The survivor is reduced to a second-class citizen because of her adherence to a minority religious faith, and therefore is under pressure to not just 'forgive and forget', but actually abandon her rights to live with her head high as an equal citizen of the land. There are great philosophical and practical dilemmas in the deployment of truth commissions when political and social realities remain unchanged for victims. The fight for legal justice often seems to aggravate social tensions locally and obliterate whatever small chances there were for reconciliation. What may appear to be forgiveness and reconciliation may actually be an abject and humiliating surrender by an oppressed people who have no other means for survival or for restoring their ravaged homes and plundered livelihoods.

The paramount humanitarian and political challenge remains of finding a path that leads to authentic reconciliation between the estranged Hindu and Muslim people of Gujarat, but one that includes acknowledgement, remorse, reparation as well as justice. There are clearly no markers for us to follow.

There is no universal set of magic solutions that would apply equally to heal the hurt, anger, betrayal and hostilities that have accumulated and been transmitted through generations in different societies and people. Historically, Hindu–Muslim conflicts in India are traced back to the years immediately after 1857 (when Hindu and Muslim soldiers and rulers fought the colonial masters together, and chose the last Mughal ruler Bahadur Shah Zafar as the symbol of the insurrection against the British East India Company), when the rifts between the two communities were engineered as an element of colonial policy.

The decline in relations between powerful sections of the two communities resulted in the bloody dismemberment of the country in 1947, leading to the loss of around a million lives and the largest displacement of human population in human history. Continued communal conflicts after Independence have been variously interpreted to be pogroms and organized genocide through 'institutionalised riot systems' operated by communal organizations supported by partisan state authorities; instigated by the political elite and biased police and para-military forces; or the outcome of weak inter-communal 'civic networks' or social capital.[12]

The responsibilities for preventing and controlling communal violence and ensuring reparation almost exclusively vest with the state. The duties for organizing processes of reconciliation are somewhat more broad-based: though these obligations vest primarily with the state, people on both sides of the conflict and their own organizations also can contribute a great deal to both the success and the arrest of processes of reconciliation. The role of human rights and the social organizations committed to secular democracy and peace is optional, but if equipped with compatible values and skills, they can vastly facilitate the process.

This book chooses to restrict itself to Gujarat, and suggests that in a major departure from earlier communal riots, where partial movement was accomplished in the elements essential for reconciliation, the aftermath of the 2002 carnage represents an extreme case in which none of the four components—acknowledgement, remorse, reparation and justice—were allowed to be accomplished to any extent. Rather, the reverse has been deliberately and actively fostered. Instead of acknowledgement, there remains active denial and blame of the victim; instead of remorse, there is pride for the communal crimes; instead of reparation, there is economic boycott and state denial of rehabilitation; and instead of justice, there is active subversion of the process of law. These profound and comprehensive failures of justice and reconciliation are the outcome of the failed role of both the state machinery, including the judiciary, and of most sections of formal civil society, including intellectuals, writers, social workers, doctors, lawyers, and their organizations and institutions.

But that, fortunately, is not the full story. Among ordinary people in both communities, there are spontaneous individual efforts of reconciliation. There is the courage and resilience of the survivors, and many acts of compassion by people of the majority community. In the daily lives of the survivors, as they struggle with the challenges of finding food, work and dignity, hatred and fear are manufactured and sustained by organizations and the state, but also simultaneously resisted and overcome by ordinary people in the ways that they lead their lives. There are indeed the glimmerings of individual resistance, of courage and compassion, of love amidst slaughter. As Howard Zinn affirms, 'Human history is not just a history of cruelty, but also of compassion, sacrifice, courage, kindness. What we choose to emphasise in this complex history will define our lives ...'

4

In Defiant Denial: Blockading Truth

Over the past seven years, as I have worked with the survivors of the Gujart carnage, I have frequently wondered if they will eventually be able to find space in their hearts for egalitarian forgiveness, especially with the healing passage of time, and whether, had I been in their place, I would have been able to forgive as easily as they are expected to. And yet I understand that they will be able to even consider forgiveness only if the people responsible for the violence publicly acknowledge their transgressions and seek their forgiveness.

For any authentic reconciliation to occur, the first necessary step is indeed truth. In the weeks after the brutal massacre in Gujarat in the spring and summer of 2002, more than forty independent citizens' reports gathered systematic evidence of the enormity of the brutality, state complicity, long advance preparations for the carnage, the deliberate subversion of relief, rehabilitation and the legal process, and the comprehensive denial of rights of the persons internally displaced by the violence. Some of the most respected retired judges, activists, writers, school and university teachers, lawyers, doctors, trade unionists and retired civil servants in the country—women and men of unimpeachable integrity and social conscience—spontaneously volunteered to research and write these reports. Collectively these findings, containing hard evidence and heart-wrenching testimonies, piece together what builds into unassailable affirmation of one of the gravest mass crimes in India's recent history.

These citizens' groups reports (which I have summarized in the annexure to this volume) elaborate exhaustively the harrowing details of the savagery. Beyond a few pages, it is hard to read, even less imagine or reconcile with, evidence of the abyss of bestiality and mass sadism into which our people stooped. The report of the Concerned Citizens Tribunal (CCT) comprising retired senior judges of the Supreme Court, senior advocates and activists, marshals evidence of how 'in the macabre dance of death, human beings were quartered and the killing protracted while the terrorised survivors looked on; the persons targeted were dragged or paraded naked through the neighbourhood; victims were urinated upon, before being finally cut to pieces and burnt. Hundreds of testimonies before us show how this manner and method of killing has left an indelible imprint on the minds of the survivors'. It notes that 'the burning alive of victims was widespread'. This is the most widely and extensively chronicled communal pogrom or riot in India. Apart from the citizens' reports there is a surfeit of print news reports and video documentation by news channels, amateur photographers and professional film makers; there are a large number of books and documentary films, of which Rakesh Sharma's outstanding four-hour testimony *Final Solutions* is the best known. There are mountains of testimonies before the judicial commission of enquiry. There is unprecedented commentary and documentation by the statutory National Human Rights Commission (NHRC), which defended the rights of the survivors of the Gujarat massacre and indicted the state for all its failures. Most of all, the Supreme Court condemned the failures of the political leadership, the police, prosecution and judiciary of Gujarat in the most stringent terms.

The few brave lamps of truth that are still lit from time to time, like the film *Parzania* by Rahul Dholakia, are either blown out by gusts of hate, or are simply lost in the blinding glitter of an allegedly shining Gujarat. The organized mob censorship by the Bajrang Dal, with the tacit support of the state government, of the screening of the film *Parzania* in Gujarat, five years after the massacre, briefly stirred the nation's conscience. The film, an intensely moving and remarkably acute recreation of the events of the bloody spring of 2002, is based on the true story of the disappearance of a young Parsi boy in the attack on Gulbarg Apartments in Ahmedabad. Dara and Rupa Mody, parents of the missing boy, heartbreakingly appealed repeatedly—and vainly—on national television for the film to be screened in Gujarat in the slender tenuous hope that it would help them locate their lost son. They maintained that the gut-wrenching film depicted only '10 per cent of the truth'. The full reality of what they had to live through, they testified, would have been impossible for viewers to watch.

This organized blockade of the truth by communal organizations and the state apparatus is consistent with a stubborn denial within many sections of Gujarat about even the facts of the gruesome massacre.

The same denial can be seen in the senior political leadership, the Sangh Parivar, and the majority of the Gujarati middle class. The position taken by the former deputy prime minister and home minister, L.K. Advani, and George Fernandes, the then convenor of the National Democratic Alliance (with which the BJP formed a ruling coalition at the central government at the time of the massacre), was that the events in Gujarat were similar to those that had occurred in innumerable communal riots, which were blown out of proportion by vested interests. Whenever he is confronted with criticism of his handling of the mass violence, the chief minister alleges a sinister organized conspiracy to defame the Hindu population of Gujarat, and to portray them as mass murderers and rapists. Modi repeatedly harps on the 'asmita' or pride of the Gujarati people—who for him never include the more than 10 per cent Christians and Muslims (who live in India but, according to the vicious canard that he spreads, whose hearts are in Pakistan) in Gujarat—which is assaulted by false allegations of the carnage.

This refusal to even accept the bitter truth—that gruesome mass crimes against humanity were committed in 2002—is encountered also in average middle class Gujarati Hindus. They typically deny with conviction the gravity of the communal crimes, irrationally ignoring all the evidence that is available in the public domain. In innumerable conversations in Gujarat over the past seven years, I have repeatedly been told that whatever violence took place was understandable, restrained, justified, even righteous, because of the burning alive of women and children on the Sabarmati Express that preceded these. This belief extends well beyond the borders of Gujarat to innumerable, eventually bitter, drawing room conversations with friends and relatives I have grown up with. In a debate on national television in which I also participated, VHP leader Ashok Singhal said that a crime of the magnitude of what occurred in Godhra should appropriately have led to the killings of tens of thousands of Muslims, and that the fact that just two thousand were killed is evidence of the great intrinsic cultural restraint of the Hindu people. The findings of the Justice Bannerji Commission that state that the fire on the train could not have been part of a pre-planned conspiracy but was probably an accident, is dismissed as political mischief engineered by wily union Railway Minister Laloo Yadav in pursuit of the proverbial Muslim vote bank. The dominant point of view adheres to the dogma that Muslims are to be feared because they are a violent people, and Hindus, by contrast, are intrinsically non-violent, a belief unchanged despite the brutal, planned massacres which overwhelmingly targeted Muslim women and children in 2002 in Gujarat, and Sikhs in 1984 in the riots that followed the assassination of prime minister Indira Gandhi at the hands of her Sikh bodyguards.

There can be no room for doubt about the planned nature of the massacres and the criminal role of the state in 2002 after Ashish Khetan, a young reporter with the newsmagazine *Tehelka*, penetrated the ranks of the Hindutva organizations in Gujarat, posing as a sympathizer, and for six months during the year 2007 at great risk to his life recorded on secret camera a number of interviews with key activists. These men bragged about the killings and rapes, about the support they received from the senior-most levels of the political leadership of the state, the production of explosives and weapons, and about the systematic planning to free the perpetrators from the criminal justice system.[1] When these utterly nauseating and numbing interviews were relayed on national television in the winter of 2007, I hoped that at last there would be national outrage, and Modi as well as the deeply complicit national leadership of the BJP would be shamed and held to account before the nation. On the contrary, the major debate in the national media was whether the revelations would further consolidate Modi's support base in the state elections that were to follow shortly. The results of the elections, which saw the triumphant return of the Modi-led government, suggested that indeed the interviews further cemented Modi's vast and passionately loyal electoral support.

This climate of denial is probably not surprising, as seven years later, I find that even the annual programme reports of the legion of funding and funded NGOs (barring some wonderful and courageous exceptions) in Gujarat tend to completely black out the events of 2002 and the sufferings of the survivors from their analysis of the issues of injustice and poverty in Gujarat that need to be addressed. Reading these reports, one could easily believe that the last major calamity that the people of Gujarat faced was the earthquake of 2001.

The denial takes a different, less extreme and overt form in villages that actually lived through the mass violence. The repudiation is not about the violence, which all admit actually took place, but that residents of the village had anything to do with it. The accepted public disclaimer that is almost universal in most such villages is that the arson, loot, murders and rape were entirely perpetrated by outside mobs, the members of which none recognize. I have found that this disavowal of local involvement is publicly accepted by the Muslim residents partly as a courtesy to their neighbours, but mostly because of fear and their utter dependence on their Hindu residents for the security to continue to live and work on sufferance on the lands of their ancestors. Privately they often deny these claims and angrily ask that if indeed the attackers were all outsiders, how did they know which homes and shops belonged to Muslims? And why did the Hindu residents not restrain their marauding? As we shall see in a later chapter, many are today courageously naming their neighbours who betrayed them, and their motive to accept the consequences of their speaking out at last is not so much the desire to see their tormentors punished, but simply for an acknowledgement that they did indeed suffer unspeakable brutalities.

5

Frozen Compassion:
Celebrating the Massacre

There is a defiant absence of remorse in mainstream middle class Gujarati society after the carnage. My first stunning impression whenever I arrived in Ahmedabad in the early weeks after the massacre, was not of a traumatized and devastated city, but instead of its strident 'normalcy'. Glittering shops, bustling roads, crowded cinema halls, people engaged in their everyday business as though nothing is amiss. Barely kilometres away, in makeshift camps in the old city, were one hundred thousand women, men and children, brutalized, bereaved and destitute—grieving the loss of their homes and loved ones in the most inhuman circumstances—whose plight seemed of no concern to the residents of the rest of the city.

Anand, established and chaired by the legendary father of the 'milk revolution' in India, Verghese Kurien, is home to one of the most prestigious higher educational institutions and rural management schools in the country. Sara Ahmed, a respected professor for many years in the Institute of Rural Management at Anand, resigned her position in anguish because of what she described as the institutional failure to respond to a calamity where 15,000 people were housed in camps in Anand, a city of 100,000 people. She points out the cooperatives, for instance, had supplied milk to the camps of earthquake survivors at Kutch a year earlier, but not to the relief camps in Anand itself after the carnage. There is evidence that the offices of milk unions in many villages in Kheda and other districts were used to organize the logistics of the massacre. Sara was also dismayed that her students were indifferent to the carnage and did not help out in the relief work. Five years later, Vijaypat Singhania, a front-line industrialist and chairperson of India's leading business school, the Indian Institute of Management in Ahmedabad, said in the convocation of graduates on 31 March 2007 that opposition to and talk of the violence five years earlier was the result of 'confused thinking', and instead we need to focus on the success of burgeoning investments and growth. He is not alone; most major industrial houses, including the Tatas and the Ambanis, have not hesitated to share platforms with and thereby extend legitimacy to Modi, despite his being credibly charged with the gravest mass crimes. Ratan Tata shifted his prestigious small car factory to Gujarat after protests led by Mamata Banerjee in West Bengal. He spoke of the 'good M' (Modi) prevailing over the 'bad M' (Mamata). But his choice of tainted Modi when governments all over the country were competing to woo him, was part of a process of legitimizing a leader many continue to believe to be unrepentant for enabling a state-sponsored massacre.

A shining exception from the world of Indian business to this complicity by silence was Anu Aga, president of Thermax Industries, who was also at the time the chairperson of the Confederation of Indian Industry's western region. She vociferously condemned the massacre from the moment it began. She expressed anguish, observing that as in the anti-Sikh pogrom in 1984, 'the state refused to act for a number of days ... and no legal action [was] taken against the culprits, though many of them are known. What is worse, very little financial or emotional help is being offered to the victims.' She added, 'Unfortunately there seems to be very little remorse for the events in Gujarat. In fact many educated, well placed people are justifying it by saying that what happened in Gujarat was a natural consequence of the killings at Godhra and for years of pampering of Muslims as a vote bank.' She observed with sorrow laced with regret that for 'selfish political gains, hate has been ignited and kept alive. History has been re-visited to keep manufacturing hate. In any civilized society do we keep recalling events that divided people or move forward to find ways to unite the communities? Will we allow the wounds to continuously fester or will we work towards a healing process?'

The burgeoning numbers of local, national and international relief and development organizations and corporate houses that contributed to rebuilding Kutch after the earthquake of 2001 refused to even acknowledge that the numbers of people internally displaced by the two calamities were comparable. In major disasters of the past, ordinary people have raised funds, in high profile drives organized by schools, offices, celebrities and the media. Their failure to do so for the devastated survivors of the 2002 mass violence in Gujarat only heightened the survivors' sense of isolation. Collectively we seemed to have drawn borders even on ordinary human compassion.

Gujarat has a proud tradition of social movements, constructive organizations and trade unions. Some brave organizations and individuals came forward to lead efforts for communal harmony, like the ageing Gandhian Chunikaka. But the majority of these did not even attempt to confront the demons of brutality in the years when they were being nurtured, or in the dark days when they broke loose. Few staked their lives to halt the death-dealing throngs; most were unwilling even to reach out and heal what had survived the torment and destruction. Their thin alibis of 'neutrality' amount to taking sides with injustice. As Martin Luther King said, in the end we will remember not the words of our enemies, but the silences of our friends.

This crisis of silence extends also to most of the political class, barring perhaps the left. Even parties built on the foundation of secular ideologies have displayed a singular lack of nerve, and of the courage of their convictions at crucial moments in our history, and have floundered in the faint-hearted calculus of vote-banks. Opportunistic compromises, open or tacit, with communal ideologies abound which seem to secure for them immediate political gains, and, at the same time, permanently erode and imperil the secular and humane foundations of the polity. The Congress, particularly in Gujarat, welcomed those rioters who led mobs in 2002, but were now sundry disgruntled elements politically opposed to the authoritarian leadership of Modi, into the party and even gave them election tickets, although they never even expressed remorse for their role on the communal violence. The Congress was in power in many local bodies and could legitimately have extended succour to the victims of the violence, but they refused to organize relief or rehabilitation for the survivors of the massacre, or even to make this an issue of political discourse in the 2002 or 2007 elections. It was only Congress party president Sonia Gandhi who, in an election speech in 2007, referred to Modi obliquely as a 'merchant of death'. There was a howl of criticism that followed even in the secular national press, embarrassed retractions from her party colleagues, and in the end hers remained a lonely even if influential voice in her party: far too little, far too late, to carry enough credibility as a marker of a national party that was willing to be counted as one that upholds the secular democratic principles of the Constitution of India.

Even the small number of middle-class residents who express

some regret about the extent of brutality of the 2002 violence still say or imply that the Muslims 'had it coming'; that somehow they deserved what they suffered. Their conviction is based on the premise of collective vicarious responsibility by people of a particular faith for real or imagined wrongs done by their co-religionists now or in history. By the same standard then, all upper-caste Hindus today bear responsibility for centuries of cruelty and oppression to Dalits, and indeed all men are responsible for the bondage of women in almost all cultures in all phases of history. Many of those who may read this monograph and most who advocate vicarious hate vengeance would not deserve to be alive, if these standards were applied to them.

Never once offering remorse for the innocent blood that was spilt in 2002, Modi has remained defiantly unshaken by the mass graves and the shaming revelations of the *Tehelka* tapes, by indictments of the Supreme Court (which described him as a modern-day Nero), and strictures of the NHRC and the Election Commission, and by the damaging findings of citizen investigations and adverse international public opinion. Instead he chose to lead a campaign of pride or gaurav, celebrating the massacre as an act of exceptional valour, as though raping women and burning alive small children are accomplishments of great bravery. In his Gaurav Yatra organized a few months after the massacre in the autumn of 2002, he portrayed the Muslim citizens of his state as unpatriotic, sympathetic to Pakistan and to terrorism. He interpreted the events of 2002 as a belated stirring of righteous Hindu impatience and anger, and the subtext was of satisfaction that the slaughter had at last broken the back of the 'enemy within'. The same tenor characterizes his speeches in other states, where his services are regularly required as the star campaigner for the BJP in various elections. In remote villages of Jharkhand, Muslim residents confided to me the terror that Modi had struck in their hearts with his election speeches, especially his oft-repeated boast, 'Only a man like me with a chest of 56 inches could achieve what I did in 2002 in Gujarat.'

The macho metaphor of the 56-inch chest (chhappan chhaati) recurred frequently in Modi's election speeches when he sought re-election in the winter of 2007. Social scientist Tridip Suhrud perceptively interprets these references to his '56-inch chest' as a measure of his 'manliness as a virtue in politics, as befits a defender of the land and its glory', of 'his nationalism, his patriotic commitment.[1] His virility,' he adds, 'is directed only to the defence of Gujarat and her people. He is also the lone man who never lets show any sign of being lonely or forlorn. As a fighter, he leads from the front, taking all the blows ... He has shown he can fight all forces ranged against him and emerge triumphant. He is the perfect male: virile in his chaste conduct, devoted yet distant, bereft of any effete emotion, zealously guarding the honour of his people ... In a traditionally non-martial culture, his hyper-masculine presence serves to allay deep-seated fears of cultural effeteness. In this the feminine is pushed to the margins and equated with weakness. Therefore, neither Modi's demeanour nor his language suggest caring, warmth, nurturance, healing or even chatty friendliness.' His lack of repentance after being exposed for the illegal and extra-judicial killing by his police of petty criminal Sohrabuddin and his wife Kausar shook the nation. In one of his election speeches he roared, 'Congressmen say that Modi is indulging in [illegal police] encounter[s], saying that Modi [sic] has killed Sohrabuddin. Friends from Congress, you have a government at the centre, if you have the guts send Modi to [the] gallows [*translated from the original by India's Election Commission*].' When he asked the crowds what to do with Sohrabuddin, the crowd responded feverishly, 'Kill him! Kill him!'

The espousal and celebration of the massacre of 2002 is reflected at its most visceral and crude in the interviews secretly recorded with the rank and file in the *Tehelka* tapes by Ashish Khetan. Madan Chawal, a local petty trader elaborates on how he was part of the mob led by VHP leaders (who were named as accused in the police complaint but were subsequently cleared of all charges when the police filed the chargesheet in the court). Chawal gloats in his graphic description of how he and other mobsters first hacked off former Congress MP Ehsan Jafri's limbs and then burnt his body parts along with Jafri who was alive till then. More than five years after the massacre in Naroda Patiya, Bajrang Dal leader Babu Bajrangi describes with relish, 'We hacked, we burnt, did a lot of that. We believe in setting them [the Muslims] on fire because these bastards say they don't want to be cremated, they're afraid of it, they say this and that will happen to them … We didn't spare any of them. They shouldn't be allowed to breed. Whoever they are, even if they're women or children, there's nothing to be done with them; cut them down. Thrash them, slash them, burn the bastards.' He further brags about the slitting open of the belly of Kausar Bano, who was eight months pregnant, holding her foetus at the tip of his sword, and then burning it: '…if you harm us, we can respond—we're no khichdi-kadhi [vegetarian] lot.' He said that after the killings he felt like Maharana Pratap.

As we watch with further cold disbelief and mounting nausea, Suresh Richard sits next to his wife before the hidden camera, as she nods approvingly while he describes how he raped and killed a woman. He says: '… one thing is true … *bhookhe ghuse to koi na koi to phal khayega, na* [when thousands of hungry men go in, they will eat some fruit or the other, no?] … *Aise bhi, phal ko kuchal ke phek denge* [in any case, the fruit is going to be crushed and thrown away] ... Look, I'm not telling lies ... Mata is before me [gestures to an image of a deity] ... Many Muslim girls were being killed and burnt to death, some men must have helped themselves to the fruit ... there were the rest of our brothers, our Hindu brothers, VHP people and RSS people ... Anyone could have helped themselves ... Who wouldn't, when there's fruit? ... The more you harm them, the fewer there are of them ... I really hate them ... don't want to spare them ... Look, my wife is sitting here but let me say ... the fruit was there so it had to be eaten ... I ate too ... I ate once ... Just once ... then I had to go killing again ... the scrap dealer's daughter Naseemo ... that juicy plump one ... I got on top of her ... properly ...' Khetan asks Richard, 'She didn't survive, did she?' Suresh Richard responds, 'No, then I pulped her ... Made her into a pickle ...'

The *Tehelka* tapes also give further corroborative, intensely damaging evidence of Modi's open support for the massacre. They also reveal that he gave his 'boys' three days to do as they pleased, and even visited Naroda to honour the killers and rapists and, most shockingly, sheltered Babu Bajrangi in the state guest house in Mount Abu after the killings, and transferred a compliant judge so as to secure bail for Bajrangi.

❧

Modi's emergence as an icon and a modern folk hero for the adoring middle classes, including the majority of his officials, testifies to the terrifying, ever-widening, engineered communal chasm. My former civil service colleagues maintain that they have never encountered a political leader of such competence, integrity and decisiveness. In the 2007 elections, hundreds of his supporters wore Modi masks as a sign of their allegiance.

A few months later, during the Uttarayan kite festival in Ahmedabad in the spring of 2008, I saw the sky crowded with saffron kites emblazoned with the slogan 'I love Modi'. A temple has been constructed in his honour, where his deity is worshipped, and a prayer fashioned after the Hanuman Chalisa, the Modi Chalisa, has become very popular; the prayer celebrates the massacre of 2002 as one of Modi's crowning achievements.[2] Many middle class Gujaratis maintain that the state has at last found its lok nayak after the passage of Gandhi and Sardar Patel. His allure extends well beyond the borders of Gujarat: national newspapers and news channels celebrate his re-election, describing him as the 'face of modern India', national newspaper houses invite him to speak at leadership conclaves, another news magazine selects him thrice as India's best chief minister, and there is wide speculation that he will be anointed the BJP prime ministerial candidate in the 2014 general elections.

Many secular commentators observed with approval that Modi had made development his major election issue in the 2007 elections. The problem is not just that his claims to a record of exceptional economic development were statistically contestable, nor that the specific outcomes were not the result of policies adopted during his tenure exclusively in Gujarat but of a larger neo-liberal framework of economic growth adopted nationwide since the 1990s. It is not even the evidence that this development was not inclusive and equitable. To me the critical question is that—despite irrefutable evidence of state-supported gruesome genocide—can silence, denial or celebration of the massacre, with implied open disdain of the Constitution and law be accepted as the only official response of the democratically elected head of the government which was legally and morally responsible to prevent the mass crimes and to protect and restore the survivors? The adoption of an alleged 'developmental' agenda in a situation of deep persisting injustice and impunity and the acceptance of this claim at face value even by the mainstream establishment reflects the legitimization of Modi's brand of macho sectarian politics, founded essentially on difference and hate. It is instructive to remember that Adolf Hitler was also democratically elected. The textbooks in Gujarat rewritten in Modi's regime, incidentally, celebrate Hitler as a leader who revived the sagging economy of post-war Germany and restored its nationalist pride. The textbooks are entirely silent about the Holocaust, as they are about Gandhi's assassination. It is this same silence that Modi adopted for much of his election rhetoric in 2007— the silence of the unchallenged victor who has broken the spirit of the internal treacherous enemy—which was even more deafening and chilling than his open celebration of the massacre in 2002.

Modi is by no means alone in his defiant absence of remorse for the carnage. Amidst the bright sparkle of commerce and many opportunities for festivities in the city of Ahmedabad during these many years after the carnage, one continues constantly to come up against astounding hate. Overheard at a petrol pump at Gandhinagar is a Gujarati youngster on a mobile phone to his friend, commenting on the earthquake that had recently struck the Kashmir valley (in 2005), 'Good that the world is burdened by 30,000 less Muslims.' Equally appalling is a conversation I had with doctors in the most upmarket hospital in the city: 'In riots, we have noticed that Muslims come in with superficial wounds, because Hindus do not know how to kill. By contrast, Hindus come in with deadly wounds: the knife is inserted, and twisted with deadly impact.' If this is indeed the case, how come official commissions of enquiry into riots from Independence till now consistently show that more than 70 per cent of those killed in riots are Muslims? But the doctors angrily dismiss this as one more pseudo-secular canard. They add matter-of-factly and without remorse, 'Whenever riots occur, and the victims pour into the emergency ward with injuries, we ensure that we give anaesthesia only to the Hindu patients. It is best to let the Muslim injured suffer the consequences of their perfidy.'

The mood is similarly drenched in hatred in many affected villages. In Moghri in Kheda, for instance, statues have been erected for two 'martyrs' of Hindutva, killed in the 2002 carnage. Further investigations reveal that they were killed several days *after* all the Muslims of the village were driven out. The story is that they were probably looting within a Muslim home whose residents had fled, and unknowingly a mob meanwhile set the house on fire. They were killed because they could not escape. Yet today, every procession in the village makes a detour to these two statues to pay homage to the 'martyrs'.

Still struggling to come to terms with the loneliness of loss and betrayal, Bandukwala says, 'My Hindu friends tell me that they like me a lot, because I am almost like a Hindu. They do not understand why their saying this causes me even more hurt. The Muslims also feel angry when I say that we must also search our hearts. I love my faith, but I am convinced that we should not believe that ours is the only path to paradise. I ask my Muslim friends whether Gandhiji would have entry to our paradise. And I tell them that if not, then I want no part in a paradise that does not admit Gandhiji.'

Fear still remains the dominant motif of a battered community across Gujarat. It takes two days for my taxi driver Munnabhai to tell me in low conspiratorial tones, almost like a confession, 'Do you know? I am also a Muslim.'

Days later, when I return to Delhi, a friend calls a local taxi stand for a taxi. The taxi owner informs him that the driver is Muslim. 'Chalega?' Is that all right, he asks.

I realize then that Delhi is not as far from Gujarat as one may have believed. Or hoped ...

6

States of Trauma:
Failures of Reparation

The Jehangir Nagar relief camp in Ahmedabad, is officially closed: the government stopped supplying rations two months earlier and the once thriving common kitchen has wound up. Just five days before, the monsoons broke over the state. Relief volunteers from an auto-rickshaw union in Andhra Pradesh toil round the clock with young men from the camp to build waterproof shelters. Almost 800 people continue to live in the camp simply because they have nowhere to go.

Twenty-two-year-old Noor Bano clutches her infant son who was born in the camp. Before the catastrophe, Noor Bano and her husband Sirajuddin had owned a handcart, sold plastic toys and utensils, and lived as tenants in Nawapara Darbanagar. They had fled to the safety of this camp with their two small sons when the violence broke out. Their handcart was destroyed and their home burnt and looted; nothing remains of it. They received a cheque for Rs 1800 for the damage to their home but gave this to their landlord when he demanded it from them. An aid agency gave them a handcart, but without working capital they are trapped and continue to live in a camp that the government refuses to recognize. Food is scarce, and Sirajuddin looks around for casual work when he does not assist the volunteers as they accompany patients from the camp to the hospital.

Halima, who has taken shelter in the same camp, was abandoned by her husband eighteen years earlier. She used to work as part-time domestic help, and also plied a handcart, selling vegetables. The cart was burnt, her employment terminated and her hutment destroyed. Against an official damage assessment of Rs 90,000, she was paid a compensation of Rs 3000. She initially refused to accept it, but later accepted advice that she should take what she was given. She has returned to her home. A Muslim relief organization helped her plaster the damaged walls, but the structure is fragile and can fall any time. She scrubs the corroded tiles, which are still scorched and blackened. There is no electricity or water supply. Halima languishes in the sad and lonely ruins of her home during the day, but returns to the security and comradeship of the camp by night. This will continue until the camp, which is no longer officially recognized, still functions. She does not even want to think of how she will live when the day comes, not far away, when the camp managers submit to the arm-twisting of government or their resources evaporate and they actually shut down the camp.

The third essential component of reconciliation is reparation. If people lose their homes, belongings or livelihoods to sectarian mob violence, any kind of healing, let alone reconciliation, is virtually impossible unless they are protected after the violence and loss, and they are in time able return to their homelands and rebuild these, preferably to levels comparable to or better than those that prevailed before the destruction. The loss of loved ones, or the violation of their bodies, can never be compensated. But material losses can be replaced to a degree at least, and although the scars are never likely to disappear completely, nor the memories of fear, loss and betrayal fade, people are resilient enough to move ahead and *can* heal if governments and other citizen groups partner their efforts to rebuild their lives.

Reparation is of course important in a practical sense because it has the potential to help affected persons pick up the broken pieces of their lives, which is imperative if they are to put their painful past behind them. But public reparation is important also ethically and politically for the survivors because it 'entails public recognition of their status as victims, public recognition of their suffering and the damage they have sustained, and a serious public effort to repair at least symbolically the harm done'.[1] In this sense, a programme of official reparation is also a component of public acknowledgement and remorse.

The major responsibility for reparation lies with the state, and the record of the Indian state after Independence in securing reparation for survivors of communal violence has been somewhat better than in preventing and controlling communal conflagrations, or in ensuring legal justice, but still the levels of assistance it has offered and its non-partisan application to various segments of survivors have always been wanting. Successive governments have consistently organized relief camps for people who were internally displaced by the violence—either those whose homes were destroyed or those who were too frightened to return to their homes. It has provided monetary compensation for loss of life, limb, shelter and livelihoods. In international law and practice, a distinction is sometimes made between nominal, pecuniary, moral and punitive damages.[2] The Indian state has rarely gone beyond payment of nominal damages; its norms for compensation have not approached pecuniary damages (payment of amounts of money that approximates the market value of actual losses suffered), let alone moral damages for non-material suffering such as fear and humiliation, or punitive damages as punishment (although a rarely enforced legal provision in the statute books does provide for collective fines after riots). It has also usually mounted programmes of soft loans and subsidies in rehabilitation packages to assist people to rebuild their lives. The limitations have been that the assistance has tended to be too small, delayed, mired in bureaucratic procedures, and implemented by not just a corrupt but also communally motivated administrative machinery which has tended to deprive the especially poor and working class minority survivors to access even what little was accepted by the policy of the state as their due.

But even this mixed and modest record was badly sullied in Gujarat, as after the 2002 carnage the government refused for the first time in independent India to set up relief camps. This meant that it refused to extend protection, security and basic survival needs to a segment of its population that had been brutally attacked and dispossessed. The attitude of the state government is best summarized by the sardonic and insulting dismissal by Modi, when he was asked why his government did not establish relief colonies. He is reported to have replied, 'What should we do? Run relief camps for them? Do we want to open baby producing centres?', a remark that arguably reflects more open contempt and prejudice than any other made publicly by an elected head of the government in India about a segment of Indian citizens.[3]

Although the state government has refused to record the numbers of persons who were internally displaced and has consistently downplayed the numbers, ironically its own defence about adequate relief efforts made to the statutory NHRC that actually confirms the conservative estimate of 200,000. The government of Gujarat claimed in its own report to the NHRC that over 160,000 persons were given free rations in the relief camps for two months at the peak, and that cash doles were given to 41,844 persons not in camps.[4] This shows that at least 200,000 people were displaced, according to the government's own figures. Even this is bound to be an underestimate because it excludes, for instance, those displaced persons who fled to other states and have still not returned, or those who were relatively well off and therefore did not seek relief.

REFUSAL TO SET UP RELIEF CAMPS

The denial of relief and rehabilitation by the government of Gujarat began in the immediate aftermath of the mass violence. Terrified survivors—men, women and children—fled to the enclaves of safety in areas with large Muslim concentrations with only the clothes on their backs. These were mostly open spaces in Muslim ghettoes, towns and villages, places of worship, schools, parks, and sometimes even graveyards. Initially, people slept on the cold bare ground under the open sky. However, as the numbers continued to grow, to more than two hundred thousand people in various parts of the state, mostly spontaneous voluntary teams were organized to manage the camps. They mustered shelters, stockpiles of food supplies, medicines, drinking water, sanitary facilities, cooks, and health and sanitary workers.

In Gujarat, the overwhelming majority of camps were set up and run by valiant self-help efforts of the Muslim community. The few Hindu camps, mostly housing people living in Muslim-dominated areas who feared reprisal attacks after the early violence, were similarly run by Hindu organizations, although with much more conspicuous state support. Even as the weeks and months elapsed, the state was almost invisible amidst the admirable but austere self-help efforts of the affected Muslim communities. After around ten days the state administration bowed just a little to national public outrage and began to supply food rations, and organized occasional visits of medical teams with supplies to the relief camps.

State authorities maintained in the defence of their inaction in organizing relief that it is the culture of Gujarat that NGOs rather than the state establish and run relief efforts. This is untrue, because before 2002, in both natural and human-made disasters, relief efforts in independent India have always been led by the state, but supported by NGOs and humanitarian agencies. It is euphemistic to describe the support for most camps in Gujarat in 2002 as even coming from 'NGOs', because like the state, the majority of mainstream NGOs which were so conspicuously (and often even competitively) active in the relief and reconstruction work after the earthquake in 2001, chose to distance themselves from this tragedy. Many of us observed an implied dichotomy in the ideological baggage of the majority of NGOs, between 'legitimate' tragedies like the earthquake in Kutch and Ahmedabad, and 'illegitimate' ones like genocide. Even more worrying is an implied sub-text subscribed to even by NGO workers that Muslims are not true citizens, and therefore expendable, disposable people or, worse, that they somehow even deserved the suffering of the carnage.

The NHRC expressed grave distress about the inhuman living conditions in the camps and instructed the state government to ensure basic facilities in the camps, instructions that the state government chose to ignore. The only state assistance to the camp organizers was a daily food ration for enlisted residents of 'recognized' camps, a household kit allowance of Rs 1250 per family, and cash doles of as little as Rs 15 per day and this also *only for fifteen days*. It is important to remember that most of the survivors of the mass violence escaped with no personal belongings. They needed some money daily for their minimal personal expenses, which was just not available during their extended residence as internal refugees in the relief camps. The facilities that the organizers of the camps could muster for sanitation, bathing and drinking water were painfully inadequate, bereft as they were of state support. The Sahmat (Safdar Hashmi Memorial Trust) fact-finding team in March 2002 found only one mobile toilet with four chambers for nearly 9000 people in the Shah-e-Alam camp. A month later the numbers in the camp had reached 12,000 but there were only eighteen toilets. Even these became badly clogged as they were rarely cleaned, and emanated a nauseating stench that attracted swarms of flies.

The criminal neglect of relief camps placed the greatest burden on women and children. In a community in which women live mainly in the privacy of their homes and follow the purdah, it was traumatic and humiliating to be exposed to the entirely public life of the relief camps. Many now owned nothing but the clothes that they wore. Bathing was possible sometimes only once in a fortnight, they did not even have a change of undergarments, and struggled to meet their sanitary needs amidst the callous public deprivation of the camps. There was little counselling or mental health support for the women who had suffered the trauma of sexual assault. They were left to fester in their memories and inner suffering, sharing occasionally in groups, but mostly engaged in helping their families survive this unremitting ordeal. The voluntary leadership managing the camps was almost entirely male, and not sensitive to the special needs of women.

The summer temperatures were pitiless, with the mercury reaching 45 degrees centigrade, sometimes higher. Life in the camps became even harder; people listlessly sought shade under the tattered shamianas or the few trees that dotted the graveyards and open grounds. The residents of the camps were even more threatened with the arrival of the monsoons. But state authorities refused, despite court injunctions and repeated representations including a delegation led by former prime minister I.K. Gujral to the then prime minister A.B. Vajpayee in which I also participated, to build rain-proof shelters to protect the survivors from the ravages of the rains. Across the city of Ahmedabad, there are a number of disused buildings of long-closed cotton mills caught in judicial wrangling, and the permission of the courts could have been sought to establish relief camps in these buildings. The stubborn refusal of the state authorities to build or requisition adequate shelters could have been because they hoped that the onset of the monsoon would result in the forced closure of all camps and establish a mirage of 'normalcy' to enable the announcement of assembly elections.

However, some local organizations mustered donations of cash, raw materials and voluntary labour to erect rain-proof shelters in several camps. Frail blue plastic sheets stretched out on bamboo scaffolding afforded the most minimal protection to the residents of the camps. But as heavy rain fell continuously in the early days of the monsoon these structures collapsed and rainwater gathered in puddles and dirty, unruly streams in the low-lying graveyards and open grounds where the camps were located.

In the two decades that I spent in the civil services, I have never observed a single instance when the state did not lead relief operations after any major disaster. The organization of relief and rehabilitation is central to the training and traditions of the civil services. Governments may have faltered in the outcomes of its programmes in the past, but the Gujarat carnage of 2002 marks a sordid first in which civil service functionaries consented to and cooperated with merciless political dictates to completely abdicate responsibility for relief, and over time even to thwart community efforts to provide shelter and succour to the hapless survivors of the massacre.

FORCEFUL CLOSURE OF CAMPS

The relief camps set up by mainly Muslim organizations were also forcibly closed six months after they were established, to pave the way for the elections in which the state government rode back to power, mounted on the dubious macho pride of the state-sponsored pogrom.

In the deluge of the monsoon, these unprotected camps gradually emptied as all except the most terrified or destitute residents left for their old damaged homes, or to live with relatives within or outside the state. Alternately, dozens of people crowded together, in small hired rooms in Muslim ghettoes. After the onset of the monsoon in late June, some 20,000 people remained in around twenty-seven camps in Ahmedabad alone, and an unknown number in other parts of the state. Unmoved by their plight, the district administration put up notices at several of these camps, demanding that they be disbanded and the residents relocated forthwith, warning that if people stayed on in the camps, the state would not be responsible for their safety or epidemics. The state government even stopped the supply of food and occasional medical supplies.

It is indeed tragic that such large numbers of citizens were forced to subsist in refugee camps, for extended periods. Incidentally, archival records confirm that the conditions of the Partition relief camps were infinitely better than those of Gujarat in 2002, despite the incomparably larger scale of the trauma, the acute scarcity of resources and administrative inexperience and personnel of a country just freed from centuries of colonial rule.

Forcing the pace of their exit from the camps threatened the residents' very survival. Internationally accepted humane standards for internal refugees require that relief camps should be wound up only after state authorities have fully restored

peace and harmony in the affected areas, so that residents feel
secure to return to their normal lives; and after the state has
completed the implementation of relief and rehabilitation
packages which enable the survivors of mass violence to rebuild
their lost shelters and resume livelihoods, which were
devastated in the carnage. Camps should have been shut only
when the survivors who sought the shelter and security of the
camps voluntarily left the camps for their homes. And till that
happened food supplies, sanitation, health care, education and
protection against the weather, according to international
standards for refugees, should have been ensured, if the
fundamental rights to life and equality of the camp residents
were to be secured.

However, in Gujarat, camp organizers increasingly found
themselves under intense official pressure—formal and
informal—to close the camps. Starved of food supplies, some
camps persisted for a couple of months with donations for
food raised by voluntary organizations. A very small number
of camps continued to operate without food supplies; they
were just primitive covered spaces that provided minimal
shelter to the refugees with nowhere to go. The camp organizers
defended themselves with stories of diverse arm-twisting
techniques resorted to by a callously hostile administration.
One by one, even the big camps, such as Dariyakan Ghummat
and Shah-e-Alam, were closed. The camp organizers faced the
uncomprehending wrath of the hapless residents who were
turned on to the streets without notice, to the charity of
impoverished relatives or to their unwelcoming and insecure
former homes.

LOW LEVELS OF OFFICIAL COMPENSATION

Levels of compensation were fixed at low levels, and these were
assessed and distributed by an administration that was openly
hostile on communal grounds to the survivors. There was no

rehabilitation programme, and negligible soft loans under existing schemes were extended to the survivors. The statutory National Commission for Minorities (NCM) noted with regret that despite manifest poverty, even destitution, among survivors, the state government returned Rs 19.10 crore from an incredibly paltry sum of Rs 150 crore received as the first instalment from the central government for relief, compensation and rehabilitation, claiming that no unfinished tasks of rehabilitation were left, wantonly ignoring the intense denials of basic needs and rights and fragile survival of affected persons. Of course, no second instalment was requisitioned from the central government. This meagre amount—the unreturned fraction of the first instalment—was all that the state government used to rehabilitate nearly 200,000 persons for six months including provision of basic necessities in relief camps, and monetary compensation, housing and livelihood assistance.

The NCM observed with regret, 'During interaction with the state government we raised the question of the sum Rs 19.10 crores that had been returned by the government of Gujarat to the government of India since it had not been utilized. Government officials explained that there were no further demands under the particular heads under which these grants had been advanced by the centre. As a result auditors have pointed out to the ministries concerned in the government of India that the money should be returned if it could not be utilized for the purpose for which it was intended. The NCM team pointed out that if more people were covered under the relevant schemes it would be possible to utilize the entire amount allotted. In the course of our visits to the camps we found several people who are in need of funds under different schemes. If the state government was able to identify such people and extend the benefits of the scheme to them they would be able to utilize the entire money allotted.'

In his only visit to the survivors of the carnage weeks after it had begun, A.B. Vajpayee, the then prime minister, announced a modest relief package of Rs 50,000 for rebuilding damaged houses. The state government's official instructions that followed pared this down to *up to* Rs 50,000. In another disgraceful departure from the past, livelihood rebuilding assistance was fixed at even more paltry levels and there was no significant effort to provide soft loans to the survivors. The state government's denial of effective assistance to survivors of the 2002 violence is testified by official data of both the numbers as well as the amounts of assistance which are strikingly meagre. The state government officially reports that it has given Rs 4.40 crore to 10,564 persons for loss of earning assets in urban areas and Rs 4.73 crore to 6631 persons in rural areas (averaging less than Rs 4200 and Rs 7200, respectively, per capita).[5] The average assistance to 2149 persons to rebuild small businesses in urban areas is Rs 6235, and in rural areas Rs 6639. The per capita quantum of support for industrial units and hotels is slightly higher at Rs 24,436 for 2083 people in urban areas, and Rs 21,284 for 545 persons in rural areas. Even this assistance is under existing schemes, and the major component is repayable loans. The average assistance per household for rebuilding homes is equally low: Rs 6808 average for 18,037 urban families, and Rs 15,905 for 11,204 rural families. It is important to remember that these startlingly low figures are based on the state government's own admissions.

The individual surveys of house damage by government functionaries minimized the valuations. A rapid survey was undertaken in 2004 of the status of internally displaced persons by the Centre for Social Justice, Ahmedabad, with the guidance of the Monitoring Committee constituted by the NHRC.[6] It found that assistance ranged from a few hundred to forty thousand rupees in just a few cases. The total amount officially paid to 18,037 families in urban areas, works out to an average of Rs 6808 per household; and to 11,204 families in rural areas Rs 17.82 crore, an average of Rs 15,905. The study found that this amount was too meagre to enable people to rebuild their homes, and compelled them to depend on the charity of NGOs or relatives. The assessment was very often found to have taken place without the presence of the affected person. The assessed amounts are also substantially less than the amounts of damage recorded officially based on panchnamas or local official estimates supported by local testimonies at the time of recording the police complaints.

The CCT report estimates that, 'apart from the loss of about 2000 lives, the destruction of businesses is worth at least Rs 3800 crore. The damage caused to private homes and agricultural properties of at least 300,000 victims of Gujarat has not been computed.' The state intelligence reports (to which I secured access) acknowledged that 10,472 houses were damaged or destroyed by arson, along with 12,588 shops, 2724 handcarts, 3110 vehicles and 1337 shops were ransacked. Even if we rely on conservative internal estimates of the government itself, it is reliably learnt (sources cannot be disclosed) that intelligence agencies of the state government assess the damage to properties at Rs 687 crore. The total government assistance, of Rs 121.85 crore, works out to 17.7 per cent of this property loss. If we reduce the loan amounts from nationalised banks of Rs 75.86 crore, the ex gratia assistance works out to a meagre Rs 46 crore, i.e. about 7 per cent. But if we rely on the independent CCT estimate, this state assistance works out closer to a paltry 1 to 2 per cent of the total damage suffered by the survivors.

The reconstruction of destroyed places of worship, at state expense, is an established principle from earlier riots. It is an important component of soothing the wounded psyche of affected people. However, this healing precedent was also not adhered to in Gujarat. Confidential state intelligence reports confirmed extensive damage mainly to Muslim places of worship: 302 dargaahs, 209 mosques, 30 madrassas, 18 temples and 3 churches. There remains deep anguish about places of worship which were buried under roads hastily constructed and tarred by state authorities, over which traffic continues to ply. Seven years later, these have not been restored. Several hundred mosques across the state of Gujarat continue to stand forlornly, desecrated and in ruins, replaced in many places by saffron flags and statues of Hanuman, described by the rioters as Hullad Hanuman (Hanuman of the riots). Many of these are historical monuments, an important element of the shared pluralistic legacy of the people of Gujarat.

PLIGHT OF RESIDENTS IN RELIEF COLONIES

Wedged against the garbage dump of the entire city of Ahmedabad is a forlorn cluster of bedraggled and grimy single room tenements. The hapless residents can never escape the overpowering stench of sewage and refuse from the ugly mountains of solid waste, often mixed with the toxic fumes of burning plastic. During the rains, garbage and sewage float sluggishly around their homes. The men spend each day in hopeless search for low paying uncertain casual work, trekking several kilometres to the main road and to locations within the city, as women plan ways to feed their families with little food or money in their stores. There is no school in the colony, and many children have given up on education. Instead, the young boys join their fathers at work sites, and the girls their mothers in the kitchens, their slender shoulders straining bravely to share the burdens of their parents.

There is an unintended irony in the name given to this settlement—Citizen Nagar—because its residents are disenfranchized in so many ways. It is one of an estimated eighty-one colonies that came up after the 2002 carnage, for citizens uprooted from their homes by the brutal violence that engulfed the state. They were displaced either by the destruction and looting of their homes, or because they were too frightened to live there any longer.

However, it is bitter evidence of the deliberate failure of the state government that it refuses to acknowledge, let alone authorize and equip these makeshift colonies with basic human facilities. The reason why information about these internally displaced people is not available is because the state government has stubbornly refused to collect and share data about these survivors as this would entail both accountability for its unconscionable failures, and responsibility for their just and humane rehabilitation.

The attitude of wanton denial of the state government is reflected in its reply to an interim application to the Supreme Court where the state government admitted, in an affidavit, that some people had not returned to their original homes, but claimed that this was only because they found better economic prospects in their new location.[7] Their official denial became even more emphatic in their response to the commissioners of the Supreme Court in the writ petition CWP/196/2002 (popularly known as the Right to Food petition), where the state government claimed that 'all relief camps were closed and riot affected people have returned to their homes'.[8] I knew this was a deliberate falsehood designed to mislead the court because I had not only personally seen and visited several of these colonies, but I had also observed and learnt from the residents many times over the past seven years about their desperate situation that persists without relief and hope. Still, in the light of the resolute denials by the state government, we felt that it would be useful to undertake a complete survey of the conditions of these colonies. In the meanwhile, the NCM undertook its own sample study of these colonies based on field visits by its members with the district officials, and came out with a damning report.[9]

The problem with undertaking a comprehensive survey was that the state government provided no list of these colonies, because it denied their very existence, and no such complete list was available with any organization. An important study by the Centre for Social Justice, Ahmedabad, in collaboration with the monitoring committee constituted by the NHRC in 2004, surveyed a sample of 4382 families who were then still living in various semi-permanent camps built by various NGOs, and estimated that the number of internally displaced families at that time would be not less than 10,000 (suggesting a population of 50,000).[10]

In our survey, conducted in October 2006, our attempt was to begin with lists of the relief colonies supplied by leading organizations that were active in setting up these colonies. The research teams were instructed to make continuous local enquires to find those colonies that were *not* established by these leading organizations, and to survey all of these. They first identified 97 colonies, but after field investigations, located 81 currently functioning colonies. All these 81 colonies have been included in our survey—58 of these colonies were in urban areas and 23 in rural areas. The colonies varied greatly in size, with 41 per cent with less than 30 homes, and 36 per cent with more than 50 homes.

One of the most damaging findings confirmed by the study is that not a single colony was established by the state government. The government did not even provide the land for the establishment of any colony.

All 81 colonies, without exception, were found to have been established by various Muslim organizations, ranging from conservative groups like the Jamiat Islami and Gujarat Sarvajanik, and more centrist religious organizations like Jamiat ulema Hind, to a heterogeneous range of small and local Muslim organizations, and in at least one case by funders with known proximity to the mafia. As the land was mostly purchased from Muslim land owners at commercial rates, it is not surprising that the locations of many of the colonies were commercially unattractive. The colonies were invariably built in the vicinity of other Muslim settlements, because it is only among people of their own faith that the internal refugees felt secure. The survey showed that more than 90 per cent of the colonies were less than 2 kilometres from the nearest existing habitation.

I have deliberately referred to these colonies as relief colonies, rather than relief camps or resettlement colonies. This is because despite their rudimentary public services, they have a much more permanent character than relief camps. Yet they are not colonies where the state has systematically resettled persons who were gravely affected by the violence. Therefore, to call them resettlement colonies, suggesting some kind of planned orderly resettlement supervised by a responsible state, would be misleading.

In only six colonies were we able to find instances of collaborations of the Muslim organizations with secular groups in establishing these colonies.[11] This underlines a grave abdication not just by the state, but also by international and national humanitarian organizations which were very active in their rehabilitation efforts after the Gujarat earthquake of 2001, and the tsunami of 2004.

The NCM in its report based on its field visits from 13 to 17 October, 2006, reflects on the dangerous consequences of this dual abdication.[12] It records its 'concern that the state was not in the forefront of the move to provide rehabilitation to those who could not return to their homes after the riots'. It observes further that 'the state government has not been involved in constructing houses for the violence affected, thus leaving the rehabilitation process to the private organizations. If these private organizations were NGOs whose brief was to serve the riot affected that would still be appropriate. But this is not so. Some of the organizations that are active in the field are not purely philanthropic or service oriented. This space that should have been occupied by the state is now being held by bodies which have a definite agenda of their own. The implications that this has for the security and well being of civil society as a whole are extremely serious.'

Our survey and my multiple field visits over the years confirm that these fears are not unfounded. Indeed, researchers reported everywhere that residents expressed great anger against the organizations that had established the colonies. Some of the dissatisfaction was the outcome of failures to ensure basic services for which the state government was principally culpable, and not the organizations that came to the rescue of the survivors when none else came forward. But many residents reported that they were under great pressure to follow, against their will, as conditions of residence in the colony, the teachings of specific sects that had taken the initiative to establish their colony, such as discouraging the viewing of television or listening to music, or enforcing the veil on working class women who had not worn it in the past. Senior members of the organizations rarely visited or reviewed the day-to-day activities of the colonies, and all powers effectively were vested in the local manager, who was often authoritarian and sometimes rumoured to harass single women. Residents of almost all colonies reported that they were required to pay money in order to be allocated the house, which seems outrageous when donations were raised because they were rendered destitute by the carnage. They had to borrow money from relatives or private moneylenders at exorbitant rates of interest.

The residents living in the colonies continue to feel insecure about their future because except in one colony, none of the residents have been given title deeds or even long-term leases to their allotted homes. This means that they can be evicted at will by the managers of the colonies. This indeed does happen, especially in the case of single women. In Ekta Nagar in Ahmedabad four widows were evicted arbitrarily because the managers and some male residents alleged that they were engaging in sex work in order to survive. It was only a dogged battle by the widows and support by external secular organizations that enabled their belated restoration four traumatic months later.

There are no community spaces for gathering together for religious or social events in 46 colonies. Of course, since 63 per cent colonies have less than 50 families, so the viability of common spaces is reduced. There are mosques in 34 colonies, 4 community centres, and in others there are a few schools. Some residents said that they wished the organizations had built more modest mosques, and spent the money instead on larger rooms or schools for their colonies. In around half the homes, the built-up area (mostly a single room and kitchenette) is less than 200 square feet, and the rest are only slightly larger. But a positive feature is that the large majority of the tenements are built of concrete, rather than mud and thatch.

Unfortunately, the survey confirmed an acute denial of public services in all colonies. In 65 per cent colonies, residents have to depend on private sources for drinking water. This often means private commercial arrangements, in which drinking water is purchased from a farmer's private borewells or dugwells, and residents are burdened with a monthly cess to be paid to the farmer. The water is often unsuitable for drinking, and it is common in the colonies for women to walk long distances to purchase potable drinking water at Rs 2 or 3 a pot. Only 13 per cent colonies have street lighting, and some of these are lit with illegally drawn electricity from a private meter, and similarly paid for by another monthly collection. Drainage is poor and often the land is low lying, causing intense flooding and clogging of stagnant water during the rains. There is some rudimentary form of sewerage in 54 colonies, common with other rural areas and slums, but women residents in many colonies confided their shame in having to use the open fields around the colony. Almost 85 per cent of the approach roads and 95 per cent of the internal roads are kutcha (dust tracks).

The NCM also noted with great disquiet the appalling conditions of public services in these colonies. They record in their report, 'During the tour of the camps, members observed that the residents were denied the most rudimentary civic amenities. They are deprived of potable water, sanitary facilities, street lights, schools and primary health care centres. The poor condition of the approach roads was repeatedly highlighted, and the team heard reports of how in the absence of such roads, even adolescent boys were drowned in the water that had collected near the village after the monsoon when the roads are submerged under several feet of water. The accumulated garbage, the slush and the puddles of water are a source of debilitating diseases, including some infectious ones.'

The commission also observed the despair of the residents of most of these colonies to find the resources and earnings for bare daily survival. It reports, 'The residents were frustrated by their inability to earn their own livelihood and to support themselves in the manner to which they were accustomed. Before the violence, many of these people were small self-employed traders, artisans or industrialists. The violence put an end to their means of livelihood since their old clients were unwilling to use their services. The impression the team received is that very few of them were employed in service. In the new environment, they are unable to resume their earlier professions and because of this they find it difficult to survive.'

This daily challenge the residents of relief colonies face finding work was confirmed by researchers in all relief colonies, without exception. The primary reason for this substantial collapse of livelihoods is the socio-economic boycott that persists in many villages and urban settlements, informally enforced but rarely challenged, under which people of the majority community continue to refuse to trade with or employ Muslims. It is hard to assess the exact extent of the boycott, because residents are reluctant to speak about it to strangers for fear of it aggravating their tenuous situation further. But I have observed this boycott in the majority of villages that were affected by the 2002 violence during extensive travels in the affected regions, although it is not always obvious on the surface. Non-Muslim employers often do not engage them as factory hands or even as agricultural workers, except in peak agricultural seasons when sufficient workers from other communities are not available, and that too at low wages. They will not buy from their shops or eateries; they are known to even avoid using means of transport owned and operated by Muslims. Researchers reported a few villages where Muslims were even barred from cultivating their fields.

The collapse of livelihoods is also because residents of several villages have been bundled into single tenements. There are colonies with people from more than twenty and, in one case more than fifty, villages. It is not surprising that residents, who had earlier found regular livelihoods in so many dispersed settlements, found themselves competing for fewer jobs now that they were cramped together into single colonies. In many colonies, we found that the residents still travel long distances in order to earn their livelihoods, mostly at their old place of residence. They work there during the days, but return to the security of relief colonies at nights, spending long hours and scarce resources on the journey, often in dangerously overcrowded taxies and tempos. This is an even greater challenge for casual daily wage workers, who may find no employment even after investing a third or more of what they hoped to earn by travelling to the work site on any particular day. It also rules out low paid work by women, such as of domestic help, because they would spend more on travel than they would earn.

The impact of internal displacement has been borne heavily by children who in many colonies have had to drop out of school, because there are no schools in most colonies. Residents confide that there remains a climate of insecurity when it comes to travelling to schools outside the colonies. Of the eighty-one colonies, only four have government schools. There are five private schools, mostly set up by Muslim trusts or entrepreneurs, but only one is recognized by the government. Besides this, children receive religious training in mosques in nine colonies. This has also deepened the divide between the children of the two communities: non-Muslim children study with Muslim children in schools in only two colonies, although there is a better mix of communities in the teachers. This complete communal divide is a realization of the aspirations of those organizations that engineered the violence, because not only in these colonies but also in large numbers of ghettoes where thousands of families internally displaced by the carnage have moved, and in the villages from where they have migrated, children will grow up with no contact with children of the 'other' community, and therefore will be far more vulnerable to uncritically accept communal prejudice and propaganda.

The residents are also highly underserved by on-going food and livelihood schemes of the state government. Our survey reveals that school children are served mid-day meals in only four colonies of the eighty-one that came up after the 2002 violence. Only five of these have pre-school feeding centres, and in only three do children and infants receive supplementary nutrition. There are subsidised foodgrain-shops in only three colonies, and a small number of people hold 'rationcards' which entitle them to subsidised foodgrains. The numbers that received old age pensions was even smaller—fourteen—whereas only seventy-six widows received pensions. Even on a casual survey, researchers found a large number of eligible destitute people who were not covered.

In summary, the state government stubbornly refused to even acknowledge the existence of these eighty-one relief colonies and of minority populations that continue to be displaced in a persisting climate of hate, fear and boycott. It completely abdicated its duties to plan their systematic resettlement in the manner that it achieved fairly admirably for the survivors of the earthquake of 2002. These wanton denials and refusals are in conformity with a shameful official policy that can only be described as open state hostility to a segment of citizens only because they worship a 'different' god.

In the colony on the garbage dump, we found children had cleared a space amidst the mountains of refuse to play cricket, even while we found it hard to bear the stench. The residents of these colonies survive with spirit and courage, amidst sub-human conditions and unconscionable failures of the state to provide a life of security and dignity to all citizens without discrimination.

Postscript: A few days before I submitted this manuscript to my publishers, the chief secretary of the Gujarat government responded to our recommendation to the Supreme Court that the state government should be punished for contempt, with both official admission about the existence of the colonies and official regret for furnishing false information. In a submission to the Supreme Court on 16 August 2007, he states under oath that 'I would like to clarify that there was no intention of whatsoever nature on the part of the state government in misguiding or misrepresenting the facts to the Commission of this Hon'ble Court. I respectfully say that letter dated 21.11.2006 of Principal Secretary, Foods & Civil Supplies to the state government, addressed to Shri. Harsh Mander, Commissioner to this Hon'ble Court, makes reference to the affected people staying in relief camps, having returned to their homes. What was exactly meant by the said reference was to the effect that the relief camps which were opened up soon after riots were formally closed in June 2002, and the affected families camping therein, had voluntarily left the camps after having taken necessary assistance announced by the government as well as one month's ration for their return. It is true that many of the said affected families had thereafter voluntarily or through private initiatives settled at different colonies. However, the state government had no information about the same at the material time in the absence of any formal documentation in that behalf. Therefore, while mentioning about the affected families having returned to their homes, what was under contemplation was that they had left the relief camps in June 2002. However, there was no intention of whatsoever nature to misguide the Commissioner by suggesting that they had never settled at the relief colonies. Even whilst assuming without admitting that the said reference was by way of inadvertence, then in that case also, the same was unintentional and hence sincerely regretted. However, it is reiterated that the state government had never misrepresented the facts and had never furnished inaccurate information to the Commissioner appointed by this Hon'ble Court.'

He adds that not eighty-one but eighty-six colonies exist, with 2990 families and a population of 20,940 residing in these colonies. The instruments of democracy can make even the government, led by a man who in many ways seems to have seceded from the Indian Constitution, express public regret, and move from denial of the existence of a single internally displaced person, to accepting that there are even more colonies than we had unearthed.

7

In Wistful Longing:
Vignettes of a Counterfeit Peace

'*I know today that I will never be able to return to my village.
And yet, more than anything in the world, I wish I could go
home. After all, my brother, one's village is one's village.* Gaonda
to gaonda hi hai. *Nothing in the world can replace it.*'

These disconsolate words of an elderly woman to me in the
winter of 2003, as she fights back her tears, are to echo many,
many times in my ears as I travel with a heavy heart through
regions that were convulsed by the violence that had ripped
apart Gujarat. Worn out by months in bleak makeshift relief
camps run by community volunteers, many grapple in the
early spell of their exile with their dread of the duplicity of
their neighbours, and gather courage to return to their villages.
No one from among those with whom they shared bonds
nurtured through generations even greet them, let alone reach
out a helping hand. Amidst their hostile silences, the survivors
bravely try to restart life in the charred ruins of their homes
and shops. Many report that the disquiet of each night is stirred
by chilling taunts and threats. Defeated, large numbers return
ultimately as refugees of hate to the safety of numbers in

ghettoes and relief colonies, sometimes fleeing in the dead of night.

When relief camps across the state are forcefully disbanded, those who can do so return to the safety of the states of their origin, but also to the dead-end poverty they had tried to escape. The majority take shelter in the tiny tenements of their relatives, or masses are cramped in small hired rooms in Muslim ghettoes, too terrified to return to the fear and hate in the land of their ancestors. Charitable organizations build homes for several of these refugees in relief colonies, but work is perennially hard to find. Sheikh Naushad returned with trepidation to his estranged village Pavagarh. 'We lived there for five months,' he says, 'but could anyone really call that living? We dared not step out of our homes, in constant dread of taunts and humiliation. If we needed to buy something, we would send our children, hoping that they would not be insulted like us.' Those who barely manage to rebuild their charred and vandalised homes with the assistance received from a Muslim charity, find them mercilessly pulled down again. Defeated, they return to the town of Halol, where they feel more secure only because it has a large concentration of Muslim people.

It is again a story I hear repeatedly as the years pass. Shakeel Mohammad of Piplod tried four times to return to his village with his family. He repaired his home with the money he got from the government and re-opened his scorched and vandalised shop with a little merchandise that he bought with an extortive loan from the moneylender. But no one outside his community was willing to purchase anything from his shop. Each night, his wife and he lay awake in fear, as drunken vandals crowed with threats and vulgar invective. Four times, in just the space of a year, they escaped in panic from their village with their children in the cover of the night. Now they have decided to abandon the land of their ancestors forever.

Women talk disconsolately of the trauma of returning to their charred and plundered homes without even a word of welcome from their neighbours, let alone a hand of comfort. Weeks and months pass since the carnage, but the people they have lived with in peace and friendship for generations still turn away coldly like strangers. 'When we look at the faces of our children, we want to cry. We do not want them to starve like homeless refugees,' they say. 'But when we hear the drunken threats of men from our village at night, our hearts turn cold, and we know that we cannot live there any longer. We may eat only one meal a day in relief colonies, but at least we are alive and freed from a life of daily fear.'

Manguben's home is burnt down by mobs, she rebuilds it and it is burnt down again. When she goes to the local official, the talati, to seek his help, he replies, 'When your house is burnt down a third time, *then* you come to me for help.'[1] Syeda Bibi of Delol village is desperate because her husband is too sick to work. Their shop in the village was torched. Her grown sons and nephews go to the village to cultivate their fields spread over four acres of land by day, but always return before dark to the safety of the town.

Still, hope has not died everywhere. Rabiya of Ratanpur village speaks wistfully of their three large shops which have been burnt down by her neighbours. 'My sons feel humiliated now pushing humble handcarts in the town. But I am sure the people of my village will call us back one day. It may take time, but I believe that a day will come when they will come to us and call us home. It is the day I wait for.'

❧

Fear routinely continues to haunt the lives of women, men and children in minority settlements. Even a firecracker sends people scurrying in terror. A cricket match between India and

Pakistan creates only dread, as it raises for them the spectre of a possible riot. Every festival, Hindu or Muslim, is no longer an occasion for festivities, only dark forebodings of a perennial prospect of brutal violence that has become integral to daily life.

Eral village had writhed in the mass violence, including the killing of seven people and the rape of two young girls. It is one of the few villages where we succeed in persuading people of the Hindu community to meet us together with the Muslim community. The façade of amity begins to crack when a young Hindu woman Sangita expresses anger at her brother being jailed for ten months on a murder charge. People complain bitterly against the courageous resolve of a thirty-five-year-old woman, witness to the rape and hacking of a fourteen-year-old child, to give evidence in court. It became clear as we sat together that peace in the village can only be bought if no one testified against those guilty of pillage and assault.

Another village in which such a joint meeting is organized is Napaniya. Muslim, Hindu and tribal men and women sit together, and we are initially heartened by the vocal expressions of solidarity. A widow then takes courage to speak, and says that her rebuilt hut had been set on fire once again a month earlier. The Muslim elders are clearly afraid that this complaint by the hapless woman would be interpreted as a public expression of disaffection, and try to coerce the widow into silence, insisting that the fire that had destroyed her home was accidental. The shaken widow still holds her ground, insisting that she had been repeatedly taunted and threatened by men of the village even since the violence. Once again, the surface façade of peace begins to crumble, as young men at the periphery of the meeting quietly ask us, 'If there is indeed so much amity in our village, how come each one of our ninety homes was burnt down last year? They claim it was done by outsiders, but how would strangers know which homes belong to Muslims? And why did not even one of our neighbours try to stop their assaults?'

No one tries to answer these questions. May be there are no answers.

෧෨

For those who still choose to return to their homes and to stay on there, it is a new untouchability that they are subject to in village after town, an elaborately accomplished economic apartheid. What is terrifying is its pervasiveness in the countryside, the fact that this new manufactured injustice is not now imposed from outside but internalized by the locals, and the unresisting, almost fatalist, acceptance by the victim community of the terms of this masquerade of peace.

In the villages where the survivors have returned, if they own a shop and are Muslim, few clients from other communities now patronise them. New competitors have opened business in every town and village, thriving on the hatred fostered against an entire community. If you were employed, even for decades, as a factory, transport or farm worker or even a domestic worker cleaning dishes or sweeping floors, you find yourself summarily retrenched. Daily wage workers who gather each day to seek work are accepted only if all workers of all other communities absorbed. A rickshaw puller can no longer depend on renting a rickshaw from a Hindu owner, and clients often openly refuse to hire a rickshaw plied by a man from the minorities. Creditors are mocked and despair of recoveries, owners of tiny catering establishments and pan shops are helpless if clients refuse to pay. Tenants of long standing are abruptly evicted from homes, shops and agricultural land.

Other forms of bogus peace require, as a minimum condition of sufferance, the withdrawal of all complaints whether of assault or arson, however heinous the crime and bitter the anguish of the survivor. Brave witnesses of rape and slaughter, sometimes women and girls, are under pressure from elders of even their own community to refuse to give further evidence, as the price of their tenuous safety in the land of their birth. The only villages to which people feel relatively safe to return are those in which they still constitute significant numbers. However, in these villages, 'borders' have been rigidly drawn. Like segregated Dalit settlements, Muslims are now permitted to live in the village at sufferance, only in isolated clusters, and the mesh of social and economic bonds that intricately wove them together in the past has been decisively ruptured. In Salia and Natapur, 250 Muslim families live together, but the panchayat has blocked their access to all public drinking water sources in the village. The people of these villages recall that their homes were destroyed also in 1990, when the Rath Yatra led by L.K. Advani (later to become the home minister and deputy prime minister of the union government, at the time of the 2002 massacre) rumbled past their village. But the hatred then had not been so obdurate and inflexible, and life had begun once again. However, this time round, the animosity runs much deeper.

People from almost every village whom I meet during many journeys report that the few destroyed petty trading and catering establishments that have been re-opened are boycotted by non-Muslim clients. Rival shops run by Hindu and tribal entrepreneurs are thriving at their expense, propped up by the boycott of Muslim traders. In many small towns and villages, people return after months in relief camps only to find that on the government land on which their humble cabins selling cigarettes, paan or general provisions had stood for decades, tribal or Hindu shop owners have now established their enterprises. There is no one, government officials or village elders, to whom they can turn for help or justice.

Those who have re-started their petty business are helpless today if people refuse to pay. Akhtar Hussain, barely recovered from a police bullet that pierced his face and destroyed one eye and eardrum, has re-opened a small non-vegetarian dhaba in Daboi village with the help of his brother. But hardly a day passes without a gang of hoodlums eating a hearty meal and then threatening to pull down his shop again if he has the temerity to ask for his bill to be paid.

The economic boycott works in many other ways as well. For decades, Muslim traders from Salia and Natapur bought and sold cattle and goats, and thrived on the small profits that they made from these transactions. Today, no one will either buy from or sell animals to any Muslims trader. Tenants are evicted from agricultural land. Farmers are unable to cultivate because their borewells are stuffed with stones, their pump houses destroyed. No one can rent a house except from another Muslim. In Pavagarh, traditionally Muslim catering establishments served Hindu pilgrims who worshipped at a revered local temple. These dhabas were torched during the violence of a year ago, and their owners now have not been allowed to reconstruct these anywhere in the vicinity of the temple. In the same village, people from the minority community are not allowed even to speak when they go to a shop. They are allowed only to point to what they wish to purchase, place their money on the shop shelf and meekly await the time when the shop-owner chooses to pick up their money and give them what they wish to buy, at a price they are no longer permitted to negotiate.

For legions of families who have turned their backs maybe for all time on the villages of their birth, survival is a daily struggle. Many women, who in the past tended their own homes or shops, today beg for work, cleaning dishes or sweeping floors in the wealthy homes of the towns in which these internal refugees have gathered for shelter. Rehana was compelled to pull her two sons out of school, and send them to work in road-side restaurants. 'One little boy brings back ten rupees a day, another fifteen. In this way alone, we are able to eat.'

These beleaguered people face their tribulations with resolute dignity and resilience, but despair occasionally does slip through the cracks. Saira, still in a refugee camp in Kalol with forty more families, breaks down: 'I wish they had also killed us,' she laments. In their village, forty lives were lost, and many young girls and women were raped. Their own shop was looted. 'We are paying five hundred rupees as rent for a small room. My husband now pushes a small hardcart in the town. What can he earn from this? I have four small children. They are always hungry. The people of my village do not even let us enter our village. Whenever I look at our humble handcart, my heart breaks. We used to own such a big shop ... our shop was my entire life. It is lost forever.'

In Kalol camp, we meet Heeraben, her face completely burnt, one eye destroyed, her wounds still raw and unhealed. It is hard for any of us to even look directly at her. She was born in Delol in a Hindu household. Her parents died young, and her uncle married her off as a child to a violent alcoholic. She left her husband when she turned twenty, taking her infant daughter with her. Fate drew her to Ismail, a cycle repair shop owner, who had also survived a lonely and battered childhood. They married, each adhering to their own faiths. On 28 February 2002, a crowd attacked their home in a slum settlement in Kalol, killing their flock of thirty goats and setting ablaze the tarpaulin roof of their shanty. This fell on Heeraben's face, burning her face and upper limbs completely. The scorching summer months compound the agony of her burn wounds, but she survives because her husband, a gentle middle-aged foster grandfather to the child of his adopted daughter, nurses her tenderly. But he says bitterly, 'Every time I look at my wife's burnt face, my heart also is set aflame anew. And why should it not?'

In a tribal village, Tejgarh, in rural Vadodara in Gujarat, the economic boycott continues vigorously against the petty local Muslim traders even today. While destroying their small shops in 2002, a spreading neem tree under which some of the shops had sheltered for generations was also burnt down. Arjun, a young adivasi teacher of literature writes a poignant requiem to the fallen mighty neem, 'You were like the adivasis: steadfast of character and generous of spirit.' In an analogy to the violence by adivasis in 2002, he goes on, 'It was not you who destroyed the shops of the Muslims. You were set aflame yourself, and fell unknowingly on the shops that stood in your shade.' He adds sardonically, 'I grieved as you burnt, but did nothing to douse your fires. Just like the intellectuals of my Gujarat.'

Meanwhile, ordinary survivors cope bravely with the unending catastrophe of a hostile government and divided people. Munnabhai, an auto-rickshaw driver, recounts his encounter with a beautiful young woman, who asked him to drive her anywhere, do what he liked with her, but give her some money. On persistent probing, she confided that she was widowed by the massacre in 2002, and did not know how else to feed her three children. The driver, himself a victim of the carnage, gave her all the money he had, weeping wordlessly as he drove her home.

At the end of a meeting with carnage survivors, in which women walk many kilometres from surrounding villages for a meeting with us at Godhra, a moment is to be etched in my heart for a long time to come. The evening is heavy, laden with sadness and the burden of stories of loss, pain and despair that the ravaged women assembled in the hall share. Just then, an activist sings out in her clear voice a song written by Neeraj, '*Ab to mazhab koyee aisa bhi banaya jaye*' ('Now let someone invent a new religion'):

> *Now let someone invent a new religion*
> *Which teaches people to be human.*
>
> *May we cultivate those flowers in our gardens*
> *The fragrance of which fills our neighbours' homes.*
>
> *May your grief and pain so affect me*
> *That if you go hungry, I will not be able to eat.*
>
> *Now let someone invent a new religion*
> *Which teaches people to be human.*

As she sings, we notice that one by one, many of the women gathered in the hall begin to dab their eyes with the edges of their frayed and faded veils and saris. Their wearied voices slowly joined in the song.

> *Even though our bodies are separate*
> *May our hearts be one*
>
> *May your tears flow*
> *from my eyes*
>
> *Now let someone invent a new religion*
> *Which teaches people to be human …*

8

Failures of Justice:
Subversion of Law Enforcement

There are many who believe that the pursuit of legal justice by the survivors actually blocks prospects for reconciliation. This is because the testimonies of survivors often result in the arrest and trial of their estranged neighbours, reviving fresh tensions. Some well-meaning organizations, in fact, have actively negotiated the return of Muslims to their villages, accepting on behalf of the victims the condition that they will not give evidence of the names of their attackers to the police or in courts. They regard such negotiated homecomings on highly unequal conditions, to be processes of forgiveness and reconciliation. Some other committed leading activists have advocated the closure of the large majority of criminal cases that were registered after the 2002 carnage, in return for the release of the innocent Muslim youths incarcerated with little hope of release under the provisions of the Prevention of Terrorism Act 2002 (POTA).

However, no authentic reconciliation is possible if it is built on the foundations of persisting injustice. The return of survivors transacted on the condition of abandoning all their prospects of securing justice is not reconciliation in the sense of a restoration of trust and goodwill, but capitulation by a crushed and hapless people. Forgiveness is authentic only if the person who forgives has the option not to forgive. In Gujarat, we are witnessing not forgiveness but abject surrender.

Communal violence and its aftermath in India have always been characterized by injustice and partisanship by state authorities. But the carnage of Gujarat in 2002 stands apart not only because of the unprecedented denial of relief and rehabilitation, but also because of the extent of the open, deliberate and defiant subversion that it witnessed of the criminal justice system, with the complicity of all its arms: the police, the prosecution and the judiciary. Indeed, this impunity continues even up to the time of writing, more than six years after the carnage. The charge of deliberate subversion of justice by the state is of course consistently denied by the state government, and indeed by the central government that was in office at the time of the carnage. For instance, the then deputy prime minister, L.K. Advani, in a television interview, dismissed the claim that there has been an extremely grave and deliberate subversion of justice in the aftermath of the Gujarat carnage 2002. He suggested that whatever failures occurred were the result of the collapse of the criminal justice system in the country, and that there was nothing unique about the experience of Gujarat. But actually what Gujarat witnessed after 2002 was not a spectacular state failure, but a remarkable success, because the state succeeded in achieving its agenda—the subversion of the institutions of the criminal justice system to ensure that the guilty are not punished.

In the scathing words of the judges of the Supreme Court of India, the bench gets 'a feeling that the justice delivery system was being taken for a ride and literally allowed to be abused, misused and mutilated by subterfuge'.[1] The NHRC earlier spoke in a similar vein of 'a large-scale and unconscionable miscarriage of justice' and stressed the imperative of the restoration of 'justice and the upholding of the values of the Constitution of the Republic and the laws of the land. That is why it remains of fundamental importance that the measures that require to be taken to bring the violators of human rights to book are indeed taken.' The failures of the state government to heed its counsel ultimately moved the NHRC to respond to the 'damage to the credibility of the criminal justice delivery system and negation of human rights of victims', by filing an application before the Supreme Court, requesting that five major criminal cases connected with the 2002 carnage be tried in courts outside Gujarat.

These damning observations applied equally to the thousands of cases in which justice has been cynically and efficiently subverted by state authorities in Gujarat. Out of a total of 4252 FIRs registered after the carnage, 2208 'summary reports' were filed with the magistrate's court. These cases were closed even without submitting them to trial, based on police claims that they were unable to collect any evidence against the accused, or that the crime itself did not take place. If this was not challenged, it would mean that one could kill, rape and pillage openly and would never have to see the inside of a police station or court room. The impunity with which the next slaughter could be executed can then be well imagined. The extent of bias of the lower judiciary is evidenced by the fact that more than 200 courts in seventeen districts passed these completely illegal orders of closure. Also, more than 300 accused were acquitted in just over a year, with very few appeals filed by the state government. Given the normally sluggish pace of justice in our country, this is an extraordinary result.

Many of the cases that were closed were deliberately destroyed, thus, at the stage of the filing of the police complaint itself. The accused were not named, and instead the violence was attributed to anonymous mobs. In many cases, omnibus FIRs were filed in advance by the police, clubbing a number of incidents involving hundreds of witnesses and multiple accused in single complaints to render the investigation completely unwieldy and confused. Often the victims were accused of instigating the mobs. Subsequent complaints by victims were then subsumed under the police FIRs, and the names of many of the main accused eliminated. Those accused who *were* charged with grave crimes were frequently released on bail without opposition from the local police, enabling them to intimidate witnesses at will. Often false complaints—called 'cross cases'—were filed against the few complainants who managed to get their complaints registered, to browbeat them into not pursuing their complaints. In most cases the arrests and the sanction of bail were communally motivated.

Investigation in many cases was assigned to police officers accused of aiding or even participating in the massacre. The observations of the Supreme Court (made in the context of the Best Bakery slaughter) apply to a majority of the cases: 'the role of the investigating agency itself was perfunctory and not impartial ... it was tainted, biased and not fair ... without any definite object of finding out the truth and bringing to book those who were responsible for the crime'. Witnesses and survivors allege that the police did not record their testimonies properly, deliberately omitting details and the names of the accused.

Once the trials began, prosecution was frequently deliberately shoddy and partisan, and it was not unusual for public prosecutors to be active members of the Sangh and affiliated organizations. In most cases the accused were not arrested, under the specious claim that they are 'absconding', while they openly walked free, threatening and intimidating the witnesses with impunity. Once again, the Supreme Court expressed anguish about the 'improper conduct of trial by the public prosecutor' and added that when 'a large number of witnesses have turned hostile it should have raised a reasonable suspicion that the witnesses were being threatened or coerced'. It added: 'The public prosecutor appears to have acted more as a defence counsel than one whose duty was to present the truth before the Court. ... The prosecutor who does not act fairly and acts more like a counsel for the defence is a liability for a fair judicial system, and courts could not also play into the hands of such prosecuting agency.'

The Supreme Court reserved its gravest strictures for the trial court. It stated: 'The courts ... are not expected to be tape recorders to record whatever is being stated by the witnesses. ... They have to monitor the proceedings in aid of justice ... Even if the prosecutor is remiss in some ways, it can control the proceedings effectively so that the ultimate objective i.e. truth is arrived at.' The court observed significantly that truth should prevail over technicalities which protect the guilty and punish the innocent, and the confidence in courts must be restored. 'When the investigating agency helps the accused, the witnesses are threatened to depose falsely and prosecutor acts in a manner as if he was defending the accused, and the Court was acting merely as an onlooker and there is no fair trial at all, justice becomes the victim.'

The injustice was further compounded by the indiscriminate arrest of people of the minority community, and the strenuous resistance by the police to their applications for bail. Men, and even boys, were charged with murder and attempted murder in cases where the police had fired at and killed innocent people, or powerful people were sought to be charged, in order to build pressure on the victims by filing 'cross cases' against them. This practice still continues. Witnesses remain under great pressure to not give evidence against those who attacked them and destroyed their homes—sometimes it is a condition imposed on them for returning to the land of their ancestors or a threat of being prosecuted themselves on false charges.

The brazenly partisan exercise of state authority is even more evident in the unapologetic discriminatory application of POTA exclusively against the minorities. Several hundred young men arrested under cases of POTA in Gujarat were Muslim and most have languished for years in prison without bail. By contrast not one of the accused was booked by the state government under POTA. With the central government's refusal to repeal POTA retrospectively, these cases persist.

The comprehensive and wanton failure of every institution responsible for criminal justice in Gujarat—the police, prosecution and judiciary—and the deliberate securing of freedom for those accused of the gravest crimes of massacre, rape and arson, from even the processes of the legal system, let alone ultimate penalties, is clearly not a routine collapse. It seems reasonable to speculate that this was the outcome of systematic planned subversion of justice in a manner not unlike the planning of the massacre itself.

There are many groups of people, and state as well as non-state institutions, that bear responsibility for the crimes and inhumanity of the Gujarat carnage and the dishonour of its aftermath. These are the elected political leadership of the government, fascist communal organizations, the judiciary and the prosecution. I choose to focus in particular here on the special culpability of one of them—with which I have served for two decades—the higher civil services, including the police. The primary responsibility of a civil servant is to uphold justice, law, order and the protection of vulnerable people. Dereliction of one's duty in a riot is not only the crime of a citizen who turns one's face away from injustice, because of indifference, fear or complicity. It is a crime of much graver magnitude, akin to that of a surgeon who wantonly kills his patient on the operation table.

Charged with the responsibility of combating poverty and protecting the rights of Dalits and tribal people, women and the working classes I spent twenty of the best years of my life in the Indian Administrative Service. I do not regret a single day of living with my family in remote, tribal districts of Madhya Pradesh and Chhattisgarh. No other employment would have allowed me to see and learn so much from the resilience, struggles and humanism of people in distant corners of my land. Like many colleagues I found enormous opportunities to implement my ideas about land reforms, laws and programmes for tribal and Dalit equity and justice, and programmes to combat both poverty and corruption.

And yet, even as I worked within the opportunities that the system afforded, I could see from the start its fatal flaws and rapid corrosion as a democratic institution. It recruited many of the country's better talents, but did little to make them genuinely accountable to the people they were mandated to serve. There were and continue to be in the ranks of the civil service women and men of the highest integrity and moral courage. But increasingly there are signs of abject, sometimes humiliating subservience, as several civil servants habitually obey without protest even illegal and unjust directions of political superiors.

In the aftermath of the grim and bloody birth of a dismembered Indian nation in 1947, the leaders of the struggle for Indian independence had resolved to retain a powerful bureaucracy inherited from the colonial legacy of governance. They expected it to act as a sturdy bulwark, a 'steel frame' to strengthen the vast, diverse, volatile land. In the decades that elapsed after Independence, a slow but steady decline set in, not only with the growth of indifference, non-accountability, corruption, sloth and arrogance, but most dangerously, partisanship and complicity with injustice and sectarian politics. One low was reached during the Emergency when few stood up against dictatorship and the subversion of the Constitution. And with the shameful abetment of mass violence in the anti-Sikh riots of 1984, the decline became precipitous in conjunction with the ascendancy of fundamentalist fascist militant ideologies in the country. Sections of the police, civil and military administration bared their active sympathies with these divisive ideologies—ignoring that these fundamentally contradict the letter and the spirit of the secular democratic Constitution of India that they are pledged to uphold—while the majority opportunistically aligned with these to advance their careers.

As a result, the corroded 'steel frame' dissolved, and in the battlefield of Gujarat in 2002, the country witnessed its complete ignoble collapse. The majority of state authorities in Gujarat not only actively connived with a planned and orchestrated massacre of a section of the population, especially targeting hapless women and children. In the months that followed, they abetted and assisted the unprecedented deliberate subversion of civilized norms of relief and rehabilitation of the survivors. They went further to assist the ruling political class of the state prevent the organization of even elementary shelters with basic facilities in relief camps, or grants and loans to aid the destitute and bereaved survivors rebuild their homes and livelihoods. This state-supported brazen, merciless treatment of victims of mass violence like unwanted diseased cattle, or like enemy populations, marks a new low in the governance of this country. It heralds the completion of the unresisting transition of the civil and police administration from protectors to predators of the people.

Until the 1980s, there was an unwritten agreement in our polity that even if politicians inflamed communal passions, the police and civil administration would be expected to act professionally and impartially to control the riots in the shortest possible time, and to protect innocent lives. There were several failures in performance, and minorities were targeted in many infamous riots, but the rules of the game were still acknowledged and in most instances adhered to. The 1980s saw the breaking of this unwritten rule. It became the frequent practice for the higher civil and police authorities to actively connive in the systematic slaughter of one community, and do this by delaying the use of force to control riots.

Why is the decisive and timely use of coercive force by the police, para-military and military contingents so vital a duty of the state in a communal situation? In every other kind of public disorder—such as labour, student or peasant protests—the broad consensus is that a democratic state must never use brute force to suppress democratic dissent. Only in the rarest of cases, and with a wide range of checks and balances to prevent human rights abuse, may the state apply minimum force to restore public order and security, respecting the democratic right to dissent against perceived injustices and grievances.

In situations of sectarian violence, however, the responsibility of the state is completely different from any other. A humane and responsive democratic government must apply in all such situations—of communal riots, or violence against minorities—the *maximum possible* force that can be mustered in the shortest possible time, while respecting and safeguarding human rights. This is because unlike other expressions of public anger, communal violence, fuelled by perilous and explosive mass sentiments of irrationality, unreason, prejudice and hatred, invariably targets people who are most vulnerable and defenceless, and its wounds do not heal over generations. The partition of our country continues to scar our psyche half a century after its bloody passage. A whole decade saw terrorists in Punjab trace their origins to the actions of the 1984 rioters. As I held on my lap the six-year-old boy in a camp in Ahmedabad who recounted the killings of his parents and six siblings, I felt broken by his pain that can never heal, but wondered at the same time how he would deal with his anger when he grows up. Likewise, the ashes of the horrific burnings in Godhra have stirred up their own poison. But it is important to understand that the cycles of hatred did not begin in the railway compartments of Godhra, and they will not end in the killing fields of Gujarat.

It is for this reason that every moment's delay by state authorities to apply sufficient force to control communal violence is such an unconscionable crime: it means more innocents will be slaughtered, raped and maimed, but also that wounds will be opened which may not heal for generations. Civil and police authorities today openly await the orders of their political supervisors before they apply force, so much so that it has become popular perception that they cannot act without the permission of their administrative and political superiors, and ultimately the chief minister. The legal position is completely at variance with this widely held view. The law is completely unambiguous in empowering local civil authorities to take all decisions independently about the use of force to control public disorders, including calling in the army. The magistrate is not required to consult her or his administrative superiors, let alone those who are regarded as their political 'masters'. The law is clear that in the performance of this responsibility, civil and police authorities are their own masters, responsible above all to their own judgement and conscience.

It may be argued that despite the legal situation, the practice on the ground has sanctified political consultation before force is applied. I could contest this with my own experience in the major riots of 1984 and 1989, where as an executive magistrate

I took decisions about the use of force, and in the former case called in the army, without any consultation. I could similarly contest this with the experiences of many other civil servants across the country, who would similarly testify that, given administrative and political will, no riot can continue unchecked beyond a few hours.

However, I will not substantiate this with my own experience, or those of older officers. It gives me greatest pride and hope, amidst the darkness that we find ourselves in today, to talk of the independent action taken by a few young officers in Gujarat and neighbouring Rajasthan during the 2002 crisis. Superintendent of Police Rahul Sharma had been posted at Bhavnagar for less than a month when the law and order situation deteriorated suddenly all over Gujarat. Following the Godhra tragedy, Rahul deployed a police contingent for the Gujarat bandh called by the VHP on 28 February 2002. Unlike the rest of Gujarat, the day passed off without much trouble in Bhavnagar. But the day after, Rahul learned that a mob of around 2000 men, armed with swords, trishuls, spears, stones, burning torches, petrol bombs and acid bottles, was about to attack a madrassa with 400 Muslim boys between the ages of twelve and fifteen. Rahul rushed there with a police force of around fifty people. Seeing that the force was hesitant to open fire on the armed mob, Rahul himself took the rifle from a constable and fired. As some attackers fell to police bullets, the crowd stopped in its tracks and faded away.

Rahul then made an entry in the logbook saying that he had fired from the constable's gun to save the lives of the children. He also gave an order that any policeman with a gun not opening fire to save human lives from a violent mob would be prosecuted for abetting murder. This gave a clear signal to the police force that their superintendent meant business and was willing to take full responsibility for his actions and fulfil his duties. This had an immediate effect on his force, and as a result more rioters were killed in police firing in Bhavnagar than innocent victims in actual rioting. Needless to say, Rahul was transferred out of Bhavnagar soon after the incident. He is quoted in *Outlook* as saying, 'I'm not one to run away from transfers. I take these things in my stride.'

In neighbouring Rajasthan, the Superintendent of Police of Ajmer, Saurabh Srivastava, with a small force and a young sub-divisional magistrate in his first charge, managed to douse communal fires in Kishangarh on 1 March 2002. It took over four hours to control the enraged armed mob of over a thousand men bent on attacking minorities, but by the end of it, Srivastava and his entourage had saved Rajasthan from going up in flames.

It is sometimes also argued that the entire higher civil and police services have become politicized beyond repair, therefore whatever their legal and moral duties they today lack the conditions in which they can reasonably be expected to perform them. Once again, I would strongly contest this belief. In the twenty years of my life in the civil service, I always found that despite the decline in all institutions of public life, there continue to survive democratic spaces within it to act in accordance with my beliefs without compromise. One may be battered and tossed around, in the way that young police officers who opposed political dictates were unjustly transferred, but in the long run, I have not known upright officers to be terminally suppressed, repressed or marginalized. On the contrary, I value colleagues, in the civil and police services, usually unsung and uncelebrated heroes, who have quietly and resolutely performed their duties with admirable character and steadfastness. Few in the civil and police services can in all honesty testify to pressure so great that they could not adhere to the call of their own conscience. It is not that there are no costs, but then if the performance of duties was painless, there would not be many who would fail in the performance of their duties.

When I stand witness to the massacre in Gujarat enabled by state abdication and connivance—or to the national disgrace of the subversion of all civilized norms of relief and rehabilitation—I confront the cold truth that the higher civil and police services are today in the throes of an unprecedented crisis. The absolute minimum that any state must ensure is the survival and security of its people, and elementary justice. If state authorities wantonly let violent mobs target innocents and continue to do this with impunity and without remorse or shame, then citizens of the country need to resolutely demand accountability and fundamental reforms. They cannot permit the collapse or subversion of the state, and its metamorphosis from an institution for justice and security, the protection and welfare of the people, into one that victimises as state policy a segment of its population, treating them as 'children of a lesser god'.

9

Diary Jottings: Living with Injustice in 'Peaceful' Gujarat

In this chapter, I extract from my writings in these seven years to chronicle the experience of living with an unrepentantly unjust state and with continuing state and social hostility.

EID AT NARODA, 2002

It is the autumn of 2002, the morning of the first Eid after the holocaust that engulfed Gujarat in the wake of the Godhra tragedy. I decide to spend the day with the survivors in Naroda, the site of one of the most gruesome massacres. I find myself in the midst of the most forlorn and desolate festivities that I have shared in.

In other settlements in Ahmedabad, there is some brave, if tattered, cheer on the wan faces of the resilient survivors of the carnage. In Batwa, in a relief camp still not disbanded despite the withdrawal of official recognition, with its frayed bamboo and blue plastic roofing, the women even produce some festive kheer, kebabs and genuine laughter. At one point, tears well up in an old woman's eyes, but others are quick to reassure her, 'God willing, next year you will celebrate Eid in the safety of your own home.'

But there is no evidence of such valiant hope in Naroda. An Islamic relief organization had distributed small packets of sweets to the widows of Naroda so that they could participate in the Eid celebration. But the boxes remain unopened. Some men come forward and offer us the traditional Eid embrace. Otherwise, there is only a pensive knot of women seated on the ground in a circle, outside the charred and brutalized shells of their former homes. There are more security personnel visible than residents. A garrulous paramilitary soldier confides to us that they have just been flown in from Kashmir. 'Yes', a young resident responds wryly, 'they have transformed our Gujarat into a Kashmir.'

As we speak with the cheerless residents, we understand the reasons for their gloom. Despite the enormity of their loss they had resolved to join the low-key celebrations, because life must go on. But just two days before Eid, the police had fanned into the settlement and burnt the homes in which the residents from disbanded relief camps were attempting to gather together the tenuous strings of their ravaged lives once again.

The policemen were armed with arrest warrants. The charges were of violence not by the aggressors but by the victims of the most malevolent massacre which Ahmedabad saw during the blood-drenched carnage. Those charged included young men who had volunteered as peace workers. Some were arrested and their bail applications denied; they said their Eid prayers behind the high walls of jail. Others were in hiding. It is this that the women are discussing with desperate, wearied anguish, beside their forgotten unopened packets of sweets.

A woman, whose husband is now in jail, says that even the police constables who arrested him from their home expressed regret as they took him away. 'Even if you regard us to be heartless dogs,' the constable told them, 'we cannot but feel sad to take such a good man to jail'. Her young son Yusuf, one of our aman pathiks—a cheerful and energetic peace volunteer—also listed in the police complaint has been absconding since. He is to give himself up after a month of hiding like a fugitive, and spend several months in jail.

'If we had used weapons on 28 February, as the police has charged, would so many of us be dead and all our homes destroyed? Would there be no losses at all on the other side, if we were the aggressors? And why did they have to pick up our best men, and that too so close to Eid and the elections?'

We have no answer. With me is Saddam Basha, an auto-rickshaw driver from Hyderabad who had volunteered months earlier to work with us in the Gujarat relief camps. He has returned to Ahmedabad to observe Eid, not with his family, but with the survivors of the carnage. Saddam's eyes turn moist as he listens to the words of the women in Naroda. 'What are they doing to our country?' he asks me. 'If this goes on, what will our country be like twenty years from now?'

I turn my eyes away. Once again, I have no answer.

SHATTERED PEACE IN DAHOD, 2002–03
As towns and villages all around it writhed in blood, hate and fire in 2002, a small tribal district town, Dahod, remained for months an island of tenuous peace. Barely 45 kilometres from Godhra, the flashpoint of the carnage, its 38 per cent minority population resident in the headquarters of this predominantly tribal district held on desperately to this fragile but precious calm.

Ten months after mass violence broke out across Gujarat, the uneasy amity of Dahod is smashed. On the morning of 31 December 2002, the local police swoop down and arrest thirty-nine young men of the minority community from the Ghanchiwada area of Dahod.

During the course of the same day, more than thirty-one houses are set afire. The tenements are targeted with surgical precision. Although interspersed with homes belonging to the majority community in a densely crowded working-class locality, only the homes of people of the minority community are ruthlessly ransacked and destroyed.

The petrified residents appeal to the police to protect their humble homes and lifetime savings, but the men in khaki allegedly stand by as their sparse hutments turned to ash in the raging flames. Since most of their men folk have been arrested that morning or subsequently gone into hiding, it is the women, children and old people who bear the brunt of the terror. They helplessly flee to the safety of a mosque in Kasaba, where an informal camp takes shape overnight.

The police refuse to even register their first information reports. In a strategy commonly resorted to by police officials across Gujarat since the first acts of violence after the burning of the train eight months earlier, the police inspector himself files an omnibus FIR of the incident. The victims repeatedly petition senior district police officials that their FIRs be filed, but these pleas are turned down. It is the local court which comes to their rescue more than a month later, and directs the police to follow elementary principles of natural justice and accept individual FIRs.

Similarly, the district collector refuses to establish, recognize or assist the relief camp. More than 600 terrified victims are being fed, clothed and sheltered by contributions raised mainly from the battered local minority community itself.

Camp residents allege that they are being punished because they ignored threats to not vote in the recent state assembly elections. As they huddle in the camp or the homes of their relatives every night, the locks of those homes which were not burnt down are forced open, and looted unhindered.

This is the reality of 'normalcy' in Gujarat, in the aftermath of the 2002 elections. For this segment of hapless residents of this dusty little town, the law of the land no longer seems to apply. Local political leaders of any party refuse to speak out for them. They have nowhere to go. They ask us where their future lies.

SECOND ANNIVERSARY, 2004

Just days before the second anniversary of the carnage in Gujarat, on the afternoon of 18 February 2004, a large police contingent goes on a bloody rampage in several localities of Godhra. Enraged at their failure to nab Salim Panwala, an accused in the Sabarmati Express case registered under POTA, the policemen force their way into more than a hundred Muslim homes, thrashing women and children with batons and rifle butts, smashing their belongings and forcing open lockers and cupboards, leaving fifty-nine people injured.

The police version is that they are responding to massive stone-throwing at the police by a large mob of Muslim residents. The FIR states that the mob was incited by a loudspeaker in the mosque saying, 'Beat the police, burn the police and burn their vehicles too.'

A fact-finding committee of the Alliance for the Defence of Democracy in Ahmedabad, comprising respected citizen leaders—Ashim Roy, Prasad Chako, Fr. Victor Moses and Zakia Jowher—visit Godhra the day after the incident, and reveal a very different story. They conclude that Panwala's escape gave the police a pretext for unleashing an operation designed specifically to terrorize the minorities, whose spirit is already broken by the massacre and the openly partisan and hostile state response.

The team verifies severe baton and rifle butt wounds on several women and children. Safiya Sikandar Mughal, a forty-year-old widow, testifies that the police broke into her house and beat her with the rifle butt while hurling abuses at her. The team verifies the injury marks clearly on her left leg and her head.

Raziya Yusuf Hochu is found with seventeen stitches between her thumb and forefinger running right up to the wrist, the result of a deep injury caused by a sharp weapon. She states that the police broke into her house while she was in the toilet. They broke open the toilet door and dragged her out and beat her up mercilessly with lathis, all the while shouting abuses. Women members of the team verify marks of beating on her back, thighs and arms. Raziya also states that the injury in her hand was caused by a knife. Her daughter Zahida, who gave birth to a baby twenty days ago, was also beaten badly and abused.

Kulsum Yaqub Abdulla Jadi, a fifty-five-year-old woman, testifies that the police broke into her house in the afternoon through the back door and ransacked the whole house. She alleges that the police took away cash and jewellery after breaking the cupboards. They also abused them in the foulest language and beat up her daughter-in-law and her with lathis. The team can see marks on their legs and arms. Her husband Yaqub and her son Yusuf were arrested. A nine-year-old Habiba Gesh narrates how one of the policemen pointed a revolver at her mother saying 'I will kill you.' She remembers the scream that tore out of her, 'Please don't kill my mother.'

The investigating team record several such testimonies, and find that the common pattern of police action has been to use pickaxes or crowbars to break open people's houses, beat the inhabitants, including women, children, aged and invalids mercilessly, hurl continuous base and extremely provocative abuse, molest women in several cases, ransack homes, break open safes and cupboards, loot cash and valuables and smash vehicles. The team personally confirms that each of the forty houses they visited was ransacked, and their conservative estimate is that over a hundred houses were attacked. They also find large numbers of safes and cupboards broken open, which gives credence to the allegations. The team points out that there is no legal basis or nexus with the reported escape of Panwala for the large-scale beating, abuse and harassment of women and children of the community who had in most of the cases locked themselves up in the houses in fear with most of the menfolk already having fled in terror.

The fact-finding team concludes that the police force in Gujarat has regressed to operating within the medieval mindset that makes a community accountable and responsible for an act of an individual and therefore retribution against a community for an act of an individual is legitimized. The aftermath of the police assault is also predictable. As with many cases of the carnage, the police refuse to file the complaints of the victims. Instead, it files its own FIR, which makes outrageous claims designed to shift the blame on the Muslim residents themselves for instigating the police assault on them. Forty-one residents are arrested for the mob violence. Also true to pattern, the staff in government hospitals refuse to treat the injuries of many of those who were wounded by the police attack.

It is deeply worrying that this incident barely creates a ripple in the national media, which generally relays, without independent investigation and verification, the falsehoods of the partisan police version. As various arms of the state openly continue to treat a segment of its citizens as adversaries, even our collective outrage seems paralysed.

The second anniversary of the massacre in Gujarat, which destroyed many lives and changed permanently the course of many more, brings in its wake no dawn of hope, of healing or of justice—we continue stumbling through our long journey into the night.

THE KNOCKINGS OF HATE, 2004

'It is usually after midnight that there is violent knocking on your door. Before you realize it, twenty or thirty policemen storm into your house hurling abuses, kicking and beating even women and children, smashing furniture, ransacking papers. Amidst the terror, finally a male member is picked up: if not a person they were looking for, a relative will do, maybe an aging father, or a boy in his teens. You watch helplessly as he is taken away. "For questioning," you are told by the policemen. You plead desperately, and ask for reasons. You are given only abuses and threats in reply.'

There is a sickening monotony to the testimonies of families whose loved ones have been detained under POTA in Gujarat. Ever since the brutal carnage of 2002, in which the state actively abetted the slaughter and plunder of the Muslim community, it is members of the same community who have been exclusively targeted for prolonged detention without bail or trial, by the authorities. Not one Hindu has been charged under POTA. There is no reprieve against a state determined to brand an entire community as terrorists. Muslims in Gujarat are living under the unending threat of severe persecution. No one knows who will be the next to be targeted.

There is some belated solace because the UPA government haltingly redeemed its pledge by repealing the law barely weeks before it would have died a natural death. Its demise will be unmourned by the secular and democratic opinion in the country. And yet there is trepidation and disappointment that the repeal has not been as effective as one had hoped. The hundreds detained without bail or trial in the prisons of our land, by a law that is acknowledged by the government of the day to be unjust, continue to be incarcerated and will be charged and tried under its inequitable provisions.

Courageous human rights lawyer Mukul Sinha, who has steadfastly campaigned against the discriminatory misuse of POTA, analyses its systematic use to create and prolong the communal divide in Gujarat. The Muslim community, badly battered by the post-Godhra pogrom, is now utterly terrorized and demoralized. Their demonization in the eyes of the majority Hindu community continues as newspapers regularly report the arrest of hundreds of 'dreaded Muslim terrorists'. The government—Modi and leaders of the Sangh Parivar— emerges as the only saviour of the Hindus of Gujarat from these 'hardcore terrorists' bent upon destroying Gujarat.

Apart from gutting the train compartment in the Sabarmati Express in Godhra, allegations under the POTA cases usually are for conspiracies rather than any actual crime. Eighty-two people have been charged and forty-four arrested for 'waging war and conspiracy to do a terrorist act'. Another seven are charged for planning to kill VHP and BJP leaders, including Modi. Nineteen have been booked for the murder of Haren Pandya. The list goes on. No one knows how many more people will be charged for allegedly conspiring against the state and committing crimes that never transpired.

In a survey of more than twenty-five cases by human rights activists, a common pattern emerges. The accused are almost invariably with no previous criminal record. Most are self-employed young Muslim men, below the age of thirty, including electricians, drivers and radio and TV repair mechanics. Some are religious teachers and relief workers. Most are violently arrested from their homes, usually at night. If the accused cannot be found, old women and children are thrashed, as confirmed by a fact-finding team in Godhra, and other family members detained illegally as hostages until the accused surrenders. In all cases people report illegal detention for anywhere between three to twenty-five days. POTA itself allows the police to detain the accused for up to 180 days, even before charges are filed.

Human rights lawyer Colin Gosalves is accurate when he says that the most unjust feature of POTA is that it allows confessions of the accused recorded by a police officer admissible as evidence. Even the colonial British administration banned confessions taken by police officers as inadmissible on the grounds that 'torture by the police is widespread, routine and uncontrollable'. The NHRC opposed these provisions, recognizing that this would increase the possibility of coercion and torture in securing confessions. This provision enables the police to torture anyone they choose to dub a terrorist, and then manufacture the 'evidence' by coercing him to sign a 'confession'. Gonsalves estimates that around 90 per cent of all cases booked under POTA are based on confessions extracted by violent police coercion.

This terrifying ratio is likely to be even higher in Gujarat, where signatures are obtained on blank sheets of paper under a variety of threats. The continued illegal detention of an ageing father who has never seen the inside of a police station, or a teenage brother or son, or repeated summons to a young pregnant wife to the police station, or threats of encounter killings, are some of the reasons that compel the accused to sign 'confessions'. More than six have sent written complaints to several official agencies of severe torture including electric shocks to their private parts, with names of the police officers, but without redress. They have also been compelled to pose for photographs with weapons and home-made bombs on the dictates of the police.

The other most anti-democratic feature of POTA is that bail can be granted only after the judge concludes that the accused is not guilty. This is almost impossible to establish, because unlike under normal law, the accused is not informed even about the charges against him or her, until the trial is well under way. This means that an accused has almost no recourse to liberty for years, whereas by contrast hundreds of those accused of murder, mass rape and arson in the Gujarat carnage easily get bail and walk free.

Two teenage girls from Godhra lost their father in jail, detained under POTA. Their mother had died earlier, and they struggle to feed their younger brothers and sisters. 'We miss our father unbearably,' they say to us. 'But now we are not afraid. After this, what is there left now for us to fear?'

But fear has been made a way of life for the entire Muslim community in Gujarat. Habib Karimi, a sixty-five-year old who was illegally detained as a hostage until his son was picked up, says, 'There may be some 300 of our boys in jail under POTA. But the entire Muslim community is under POTA in Gujarat in their homes.'

The half-baked repeal of POTA *without retrospective effect* that has been effected by the UPA government will not secure freedom for his son, and hundreds of others incarcerated for years without trial. The BJP announced its resolve to promulgate laws like POTA in the states that they govern. The UPA government even says that it will introduce some provisions of the Terrorist and Disruptive Activities (Prevention) Act into existing law. Elementary justice remains mortally threatened in democratic India.

THE ETHICS OF COLLECTIVE VENGEANCE, 2005
Some of the most brutal mass crimes in recent history are those of collective vengeance against an entire community for the real or imagined crimes of a few of its members. The blood of thousands of innocent Sikhs flowed in 1984 as a reprisal against the perfidy of two Sikhs guards who assassinated Indira Gandhi. Terrorist attacks on the twin towers in New York have been used to condone indefensible military attacks on civilian populations in Afghanistan and Iraq.

The same dangerously warped and morally flawed logic that was used to condone the merciless bloodletting that mortally wounded Gujarat in 2002. Modi described the gruesome incident at Godhra as a pre-planned 'one sided collective terrorist attack by one community...'. In the BJP parliamentary party meeting in Delhi in December 2002, the then prime minister, A.B. Vajpayee, lamented in a thinly disguised rationalization of the 'Hindu anger' manifested in the violence that followed the alleged torching of the train, 'Why didn't people of the Muslim community condemn the Godhra incident? Even today, there is no repentance that we committed a mistake or that this should not have happened and that it was a crime.' [1] The poet prime minister suggested that Muslims as a whole should seek forgiveness for the crime that some of their co-religionists had allegedly committed.

Ever since then, intolerably heavy burdens of vicarious guilt have been thrust upon the shoulders of the entire Muslim community in India for the alleged outrage by a few who shared their religious faith in Godhra. The slaughter, rape, loot and arson that followed were widely perceived as righteous, or at least an understandable reaction to the 'barbaric crime' of the Muslims. Despite the Banerjee Commission categorically proving that the fire was an accident, the same 'logic' reverberates to this day in middle-class living rooms across the country. Equivalent reasoning choked the flow of human sympathy for the brutalized, bereaved and homeless survivors of the Gujarat carnage. Unlike the tsunami two years later, there was no jostling of celebrities, no star-studded concerts, no media houses and newspaper houses competing to raise money for the victims, only a deafening silence. The unstated sub-text was that it was somehow fitting that a gravely tainted community was left to deal with the consequences of its collective transgressions.

It is particularly striking that this doctrine of collective communal responsibility for crimes of individuals is applied only selectively. For the recent gruesome killing of Dalits in Jhajjar in Haryana, or indeed in instances of atrocities on Dalits that shame every generation, the upper-caste Hindu majority are never held collectively responsible. Nor are they pronounced jointly guilty for the massacres of 1984 and 2002. Such collective responsibility seems apportioned only to minorities.

The official version of the government of Gujarat, interpreted through nine charge-sheets, is that a conspiracy was hatched at a guesthouse in Godhra, the night before the fire, to kill the kar sewaks returning from Ayodhya, by setting aflame coach S-6 of the Sabarmati Express. For this, 140 litres of petrol were said to have been procured. The next morning, on 27 February 2002, the train was halted at Godhra station by the conspirators, by repeatedly pulling the alarm chain. It is conceded in the police version that a kar sewak misbehaved with a Muslim girl which led to tension and confusion. It is alleged that taking advantage of the confusion the conspirator cut through the canvas of the vestibule, allowed the petrol to leak in coach number S-6 and then set it aflame.

However, the evidence before the Shaha, Nanawati and Banerjee judicial commissions, and reports of independent experts, completely debunks the police theory. There is no explanation as to how the alleged conspirators came to know that kar sewaks were travelling by the Sabarmati Express on that fateful day, when the police and intelligence departments themselves consistently claim they had no such advance information. It is established that it was not Muslims but the kar sewaks who pulled the chain to stop the train, because several passengers were left behind on the platform. The theory of petrol being poured into the bogey also collapses because none of the seventy or more passengers who escaped from the bogey had any burn wounds below their waist.

Although the evidence now overwhelmingly supports the theory of an accidental fire within the train, and death mainly by asphyxiation, there are still many unanswered questions that the investigations and history will hopefully answer. However, an impartial assessment of the large body of available evidence makes one thing incontrovertible, and this is that the official version of a conspiracy by the Ghanchi Muslims of Godhra to set the bogey aflame, is unsupported by any credible corroboration.

The carefully reasoned Banerjee interim report has exposed the venality and cynicism of state authorities who created and continue to expound stubbornly this communally incendiary and pernicious Muslim conspiracy theory, which has profoundly impaired communal relations across the country, and further demonized the entire Muslim community.

However, it is perilous to argue that the Bannerjee Commission report has also demolished the ethical justification for the 2002 massacre of minorities in Gujarat, because such justification never existed. No community can be held collectively culpable for the crimes of individuals.

A VILLAGE 'CLEANSED', 2005

Moghri, in the outskirts of Kheda, is one of a growing number of villages in Gujarat which have been proudly cleansed by the militant Hindutva movement of their erstwhile Muslim populations. Around ninety Muslim families lived there for generations before 2002. In the tempest of hate in 2002, they were driven out, destitute and in terror, never to return. Most families owned agricultural land; the homes of those families who owned these properties were torched. For Muslim tenants of Hindu house-owners, the houses themselves were spared, but their properties were looted and burned.

In the months that followed, some attempted sporadically and fearfully to return to their ravaged homes and lands, but the villagers openly told them that they were unwelcome and that their security could not be assured. They warned them that the first condition for anyone who still wanted to return to the village of their birth was that they could not give evidence in any police investigation or court trial into the mass crimes of 2002.

Only one timid resident agreed to these humiliating terms. He filed no case and refused to name his tormentors to policemen and magistrates. Eighteen months after the massacre, the elders of Moghri village agreed grudgingly to permit his homecoming. He hired a truck and returned with his family to what remained of his home. Two days later, he fled after a mob gathered outside his home, threatening to set it aflame once again demanding that he pressurise other villagers into withdrawing their cases. Eight days later, the truck returned forlornly to collect his belongings once again. He later bought a home in a settlement with 98 per cent Muslims. He then joined other survivors of the carnage to file a complaint before a magistrate against those who threatened him.

The villagers have filed a total of eight complaints in the magistrate's courts against the mass crimes of 2002, and four more for the threats that followed. But predictably the police have done little to investigate the crimes. In exile from their village, many survivors live in small tenements in Muslim ghettoes built by Islamic relief organizations. But they are too frightened to cultivate their fields, and the economic boycott robs them of opportunities to earn a livelihood. Many have been compelled to sell their lands at distress prices to Hindu land-owners, letting go off their last hope of ever returning home.

ZAHIRA: VICTIM AS VILLAIN, 2006

A young woman, barely twenty years old, who lost fourteen members of her family in the 2002 violence, has desolately spent the last four months in a prison ward in Nasik. Once a shining symbol of the struggle for justice in Gujarat, today she sits in her cell abandoned, disgraced in public opinion and condemned by the Supreme Court for contempt of a one year sentence, extendable by three months—the highest such sentence for misleading and thereby causing disrespect to the courts probably in post-Independence judicial history. Her name is Zahira Sheikh.

There is no doubt that Zahira changed her statement repeatedly in court, and thereby endangered the process of justice, and in doing so faltered ethically. But it must be remembered that in contrast to most 'hostile' witnesses who lied to the courts in cases like the Jessica Lal murder, Zahira was and remains, first and foremost, a victim. Recall by contrast, for instance, the penalty imposed on the then chief minister of UP, Kalyan Singh, for wantonly reneging on his assurance before the court that his government would protect the Babri Masjid, which shamed the nation and left thousands dead and unhealed scars on the national psyche. His punishment extended just to the period up to the rising of the court. Zahira was sixteen when mobs slaughtered fourteen members of her extended family in Vadodara. Since then, she has struggled and tried to survive extremely difficult circumstances as best as she could.

More than anything else, Zahira's failures are the outcome of the wilful and comprehensive subversion of justice, and all those who are responsible to secure it. There is no statutory witness protection scheme to shield vulnerable witnesses like Zahira, and the police did nothing to restrain those who continue to terrorize witnesses at will.

It is not surprising that in such circumstances the police was able to 'close' more than 2000 cases without even submitting them to trial. An estimated 200 judges in seventeen districts were willing partners in this slaughter of the judicial process. A persistent legal battle in the Supreme Court has led to the eventual reopening of almost all these cases for investigation, which is in itself an affirmation of this unprecedented and spectacular governmental and judicial subversion of justice, yet no court has thought it fit to punish the police officers and judges.

For the few cases that went to trial, public prosecutors were appointed from the Sangh, who deliberately weakened the cases so the majority of the accused were acquitted. My team of human rights workers and I have personally witnessed judges even today openly encouraging extra-legal 'compromises' outside court. The most recent such instance is in Belol village in Kheda, where the judge reprimanded human rights activists for *preventing* the state efforts to turn the witnesses hostile. There is no provision for 'compromise' for grave crimes in the Indian Penal Code, yet judges, lawyers and prosecutors in Gujarat openly support efforts to force witnesses to rescind on their complaints and statements.

The matter of victimized witnesses turning 'hostile' in Gujarat is not a simple one of greed. It is of negotiating survival in the aftermath of a massacre, where the state and its agencies, refuse to protect the rights of victims to security and equal citizenship.

Zahira's choices are by no means defensible. But would many of us in her situation as a traumatized and bereaved young woman facing extreme state-supported hostility and impunity, intimidation and inducements, and a shamelessly partisan criminal justice system, have fared much better than her?

WAGES OF HATE: REPLAY 2006

A numbing spiral of violence has once again gripped Vadodara, a city that was brutally torn apart by the mass murder of many of its citizens in 2002. Large parts of the city are engulfed by the tense unquiet of curfew. The streets are emptied of people, except clutches of homeless families to whom no curfew can apply. Instead, convoys of security forces man the roads, and bleary-eyed policemen have set up pickets in a belated claim to guard the people of the beleaguered city.

Yet the faith of many citizens in the desire and ability of the state administration to protect them and restore peace and secure justice is completely decimated, more so because the violence was provoked and stoked directly by the openly sectarian and provocative actions of the municipal and police administration.

The dispute was over the declared resolve of the local government to demolish a dargah of Sufi saint Hazrat Rasiuddin Chisti. The newly elected city council, with an overwhelming BJP membership, voted for its removal, claiming that it was an 'encroachment' and obstructed traffic, despite the fact that the shrine was close to the pavement and the flow of traffic was constrained by the adjacent narrow Champaner Darwaza.

The worried leaders of the Muslim community tried to negotiate with the mayor and councillors. Realizing that the administration was adamant, they agreed to demolish substantial parts of the structure and canopy of the dargah themseles, and retain only a small structure over the actual grave. However, their conciliatory offer of compromise was rejected and the council decided that it would settle for nothing less than a full demolition. The mayor, accompanied by BJP leaders notorious for their role in the 2002 massacre, municipal authorities, and a large contingent of armed policemen descended on the dargah with bulldozers. Local Muslim youths quickly mobilized peaceful resistance by a sit-in around the site while the mayor and the mob raised inflammatory slogans. The peaceful demonstrators soon found themselves pelted with stones, and being shot at.

Television cameras recorded how policemen shot at the retreating crowd at point-blank range, aiming at their heads rather than their feet. Two men died and many were injured in the resultant chaos. All rules that regulate the use of force against civilian populations were disregarded: there was no advance warning, no lathi charge, no water cannons, no rubber bullets, no shooting at the feet. There was firing to kill.

The municipal administration and mob then demolished the Sufi shrine, and immediately built a road over it. Their triumphant mood revived memories of the Babri Masjid demolition and that of the razing of the Wali Gujarati dargah in Ahmedabad in 2002, except that this operation was openly planned and executed by the state administration itself.

The authorities countered the widespread dismay and outrage that followed by describing the demolition as part of a routine administrative exercise to widen roads and 'beautify' the city. They claimed that several temples had similarly been peacefully demolished with no protest, thus implying that the Muslims were violent and opposed to development. This communal subterfuge was uncritically relayed by large sections of the media, and remains the popular perception of the violent events in Vadodara, because it fits and fuels prevailing communal stereotypes.

What the authorities neglected to mention was that the Hindu temples that were demolished were mostly 'deras' or tiny private temples built in recent years. We took photographs of at least twenty temples, mostly in the vicinity of police stations—one stood proudly on the premises of the police commissioner's office—or the municipal headquarters that indeed blocked the roads, but there was no demand or move to demolish these temples. Further, at least two much more substantial Muslim shrines had also been demolished, with no protest by the Muslim community.

There is evidence that this dargah was several hundred years old, and probably it predated the city of Vadodara itself. Therefore, by no definition can it be described as an encroachment. If at all, it was the city that had encroached on the shrine! There are records of a city survey undertaken in 1912 by the erstwhile Gaekwad ruler, copies of which we acquired, that clearly indicate the presence of the shrine. An act of Parliament, passed after the traumatic demolition of the Babri Masjid in 1992, says that the status quo of religious structures that existed in 1947 cannot be altered. This makes the officially sanctioned demolition not only communally motivated, but also in violation of the law of the land.

Tension mounted further when a young man was cruelly burnt alive in his car by the crowds that gathered unhindered around the site despite curfew. Television footage records ghoulish celebrations of dancing, cheering men around the car as the young man slowly burnt to death. Repeated entreaties on telephone for protection to police officers were ignored. A retired police officer testifies that he lay down on the road before a passing fire engine to persuade it to douse the fire in the car, but the driver refused and drove away in reverse gear.

In a gruesome replay of the tragic events of 2002, mobs gathered under the aegis of the police to stone and burn Muslim homes and properties. We met fifteen working class Muslim young men who testified to being shot at by policemen at point blank range. This time round, there was also some retaliatory violence against the Hindu community, and two men were stabbed to death. Fortunately, widespread television coverage and the firm stance taken by the central UPA government (for the first time in the context of the continuing injustice in Gujarat) mercifully helped avert a full recurrence of the events of 2002.

PSEUDO-MYTHOLOGY OF SHABRI KUMBH IN GUJARAT, 2006

The tribal people in the vast forested tracts in the interiors of India today face a grave new hazard. They are already dispossessed of their lands and forests, and grappling desperately with endemic exploitation. In their bleak daily destiny of debt, bondage and hunger, the rapid incursions of radical Hindutva, systematically being propagated by the

Sangh, threaten to divide and communalize tribal communities and distance them further from struggles for justice.

For a majority of tribal people, the Muslim is invisible. The 'enemy' invented for them instead by the Sangh is Christianity, demonized not as a faith founded on compassion and service, but as a dangerous foreign conspiracy to destabilize the existing social order, propagated by 'fraudulent' missionaries, pastors and nuns. Their health and educational services are dismissed as bribes for conversion. A.B. Vajpayee, with his characteristic ambiguity, would call for a 'national debate on conversions' whenever the unseen violence of the everyday erupted as attacks on missionaries or places of worship.

In Gujarat, the epicentre of the battle against Christianity lies in the district Dangs, with 92 per cent tribal population, mainly Bhils and Warlis. This impoverished district gained notoriety in 1998, during which thirty-eight acts of violence were recorded against the tiny population of a few thousand people and pastors in the district, and places of worship. Independent investigations revealed that these attacks were the result of systematic hatred and suspicion bred among local adivasis by activists of Sangh organizations like Vanvasi Kalyan Ashram and Hindu Jagran Manch. Fear again mounts because of the Sangh's energetic plans to organize a mammoth Shabri Kumbh in Dangs in February 2006.

There have been a series of such massive gatherings of tribal people and Hindutva activists in the region in recent years, including a Vishal Hindu Mahasangam in the Bhil district Jhabua in neighbouring Madhya Pradesh in 2002, and another Kumbh in Bhilwada in Rajasthan in 2004. Each of these gatherings is preceded by intensive mobilization by Sangh activists in tribal households, wide distribution of lockets and statues of Hindu gods like Hanuman, and vicious door-to-door propaganda against the minorities. The choice of Hindu icons for adivasi areas is also instructive. These are Hanuman and Shabri, revered as loyal servant rather than masters in their own right like Ram. There are numerous programmes, fashioned as 'ghar vapsi' or homecomings, or alleged re-conversions by tribal people to the Hindu faith. Each of these gatherings has left a trail of violence and enduring fear among Christian adivasis, and massive expansion in electoral support for the BJP.

However, as both anthropologists and district gazetteers testify, the local adivasis are not originally Hindu, especially not of the narrow Brahmanical version of the faith purveyed by Sangh activists. Their worship is animistic: they pray to the tigers and cows, serpents and the moon, the hills and forests, the wind and the rains. Their gods are appeased by animal sacrifice and offerings of home-brewed liquor, amidst dance and celebration.

The modus operandi of Hindutva activists is to adopt and gradually co-opt these tribal gods who are gradually converted to teetotallers and vegetarians and reinvented as local versions of mainstream Hindu gods. Temples are built to these 'Hindu' deities, and Hindu festivals introduced with large mobilization. Their base is consolidated through service activities by Sangh organizations, especially in primary education, supported generously by overseas Hindus. These Sangh schools, including Ekal Vidyalayas and Saraswati Shishu Mandirs, systematically consolidate both a detribalized Hindu identity for the adivasis, and hatred for the 'foreign' faiths—Christianity and Islam.

This is precisely the strategy behind the Shabri Kumbh. The story goes that Ram came across Shabri in his search for Sita and ate the berries that she tasted to check their sweetness. As with Ayodhya, Hindutva activists claim sudden precise knowledge of the exact location where Ram encountered Shabri, and decide to organize the Kumbh there. Ironically, there is religious sanction for only four Kumbhs at fixed locations in twelve-year cycles, unchanged through the millennia. The plans for the Shabri Kumbh are thus based on cynically manipulated mythology, for narrow sectarian objectives of terrorizing further the small population of a few thousand adivasi Christians, and to promote a false majoritarian Hindu identity in violent opposition to them.

What causes further dismay is the open support of the state government to the activities of the Sangh. All pretence of boundaries separating them has been abandoned. The Kumbh is being openly organized by the Sangh, and massive development funds in one of the poorest districts of the country are being diverted for constructing roads, platforms and check dams for the water reservoir in which people will bathe in the Kumbh. The local administration refuses action against the Sangh pamphlets and CDs which repeatedly refer to the church in derogatory terms, and ignores the terror mounting in the Christian adivasi population, as well as destruction of the fragile environment. Instead, the collector defends these as legitimate religious activities, with the added benefits of 'development'.

This openly partisan support of the state government for the dangerous sectarian objectives of the Sangh needs to be combated, and the safety of minorities secured. Else the tribal regions of India, already dispossessed and frequently in violent turmoil, will flow bitterly with the blood of sectarian hatred.

COUNTERFEIT ENCOUNTERS AND THE 'NATION', JUNE 2007

The current wave of outrage in the country over the horrific murders of Sohrabuddin and Kauserbi by Vanjara and his men in khaki in Gujarat is likely to be transient, a passing squall. The dust that it raises will rapidly settle, and we will forget, in the same way as we have expelled from memory so many similar inequities in the recent past: the women who stripped themselves naked in anguish in Manipur to protest the violations of security forces, the staged killings of innocents as militants in Kashmir, the mass cremations of thousands of young men who were abducted by the police and later dubbed Khalistani extremists in Punjab in the troubled 1980s, counterfeit encounter killings of alleged Naxalite sympathizers in the backwaters of rural ferment and oppression for decades in Andhra Pradesh, Bihar and Chattisgarh, and bogus encounters with alleged terrorists in the country's capital. Even less do we even register the routine killings of the poorest tribals or Dalits, after torture and extortion in rural police outposts, or numerous judicial commissions of enquiry that testify to the open participation of men in uniform in the slaughter of minorities in communal riots.

The Central Bureau of Investigation, in 1996, submitted a report to the Supreme Court that established that in just three crematoria of Amritsar, as many as 2097 illegal cremations were carried out by security forces between 1984 and 1995. An independent human rights investigation established that the illegal disposal of bodies by security forces was not confined to just three crematoria of Amritsar. Disappearances occurred in all districts of Punjab. In nearly 60 per cent cases, the person who 'disappeared' was subsequently reported to have died in a police 'encounter'. The victims included doctors, lawyers, journalists, students, businessmen, and even government civil servants. In over 25 per cent cases, the police not only took away the victim; it also destroyed, damaged, and confiscated family property. In an equal number of incidents, the police abducted and killed more than one member of the same family. The police routinely refused to inform the victims' families, and extorted money from them.

The Supreme Court referred the matter to the NHRC, and did nothing when the commission took a minimalist interpretation of its ambit. After ten years of tortuous proceedings, pursued resolutely by the devastated families of the victims and supported by dedicated human rights defenders like Indira Jaising, Ram Narayan Kumar, Sukhman and Ashok Agarwal, the commission refused in the end to hold any officer or agency accountable for the violations, and declined to investigate disappearances, extra-judicial executions, custodial deaths and illegal cremations throughout Punjab.

In Andhra Pradesh, again for a decade, a committee of concerned citizens, convened by S.R. Sankaran, have tirelessly pressed for the deployment of moral, democratic and legal instruments to try to stem the unending brutal spiral of violence that has seized many impoverished districts of Telengana. They observe that the state continues to portray the Naxalite movement as a law and order problem, and refuses to recognize it as an expression of people's aspirations to a life of dignity and equality. The state response remains violent, including physically liquidating hundreds, mainly young men, in encounters. The committee finds that these 'encounter killings are not isolated aberrations or unintended transgressions of law by individual police personnel' but a deliberate response of the state to crush a complex societal problem through indiscriminate killings. It concludes that 'encounters introduce terror as a component of governance and erode its very democratic essence'.

Unfortunately, there are few who heed these voices of humanity. In Gujarat, in response to a question from a member of the assembly, as many as twenty-one encounter killings by the state police were reported between 2003 and 2006. But the list submitted by the Gujarat government did not include the names of Sohrabuddin and Kauserbi. A murky cloud of official secrecy continues to deliberately cloud the numbers and circumstances of encounter deaths caused by the Gujarat state police.

However, even this limited official report again raises disturbing questions. Six of those killed were already in police custody, and it is incredible that they could possess firearms in custody to warrant killing by the police in self defence. In one case, the police claim that two policemen fired six rounds to kill a man with a revolver. There was no post mortem, or statutory magisterial enquiry. There are no materials to even subsequently justify the inference that they were terrorists or grave offenders. All these facts were brought to the notice of the Supreme Court in a petition in early 2007 by B.G. Verghese and lawyer Nitya Ramakrishnan, but the court did not find 'enough basis' to order an enquiry into the encounter killings.

Each nation must strike a fine ethical and political balance between protecting its interests and the rights of its people. In India, the choice of the executive, and even the judiciary, has tilted mostly in favour of permitting the uniformed forces to break the law of the land with impunity, even to kill, especially in times of perceived threats to national integrity—cheered along by most segments of the middle classes. Policemen themselves often claim that they are motivated by a higher love for the nation. Many are, but not those who kill unarmed people in defiance of the law of the land. K.P.S. Gill, who led the security forces in Punjab in the decisive 'bullet for bullet' campaign against militancy of the late 1980s, describes his forces as men who 'fight and die for India' and 'who risked their lives in defence of the state'. The disgraced Gujarat police officer Vanjara also fashions his encounter killings as 'deshbhakti' (patriotism), and claims that with his arrest, 'the battle lines are drawn', presumably in his war against the Muslim community, which is of course viciously demonized as terrorists implacably unfaithful to their motherland. L.K. Advani, as the union home minister in 2001, announced in Punjab that his government was 'contemplating steps to provide legal protection and relief to the personnel of the security forces facing prosecution for alleged excesses during anti-insurgency operations' in Punjab, Kashmir and the North East.

Faked killings by men in khaki are not aberrations of a few runaway miscreant police officers; it is an integral, if shadowy, element of the system itself, one in which the state eliminates people outside the process of the law, as an instrument to tame civic dissent. These bullets indeed crush, with state terror and lawlessness, the weakest and most disenfranchised of our people, particularly if they are restive—religious and ethnic minorities, Dalits and tribal people, agricultural workers and slum dwellers.

We may forget and move on, but for those whose loved ones were felled by furtive bullets fired by agents of a democratic state that functions lawlessly, there will be no closure or healing. It is only truth, however ugly, told with unflinching honesty, which would heal their agony. For this to happen, the leaders, the courts and the people of this land need to stand tall on the side of justice for no nation is genuinely secure on foundations of injustice.

10

Fighting Back:
Legal Resistance to Injustice

Although the aftermath of the carnage in Gujarat in 2002 has witnessed the most elaborate deliberate subversion of justice by the government in independent India, it has also witnessed some of the most effective resistance put up by the civil society and human rights activists, and moments of unprecedented judicial pronouncements, indictment and remedies by the Supreme Court of India and by the NHRC.

There have been diverse strategies that survivors and human rights defenders have adopted in their search for justice. The preferred strategy of organizations like Citizens for Peace and Justice, Foundation for Civil Liberties, Centre for Social Justice, Jan Vikas, Human Rights Law Network and the Commonwealth Human Rights Initiative has been to take up a small number of selected cases of large massacres, and to fight these with the best available legal talent and financial resources for witness protection. This has met with outstanding success and impact. This strategy was deployed most notably in the Best Bakery case spearheaded with great resolution and force by the Citizens for Peace and Justice led by human rights' defender and journalist Teesta Setalvad. The case drew enormous national attention to the grave injustices and subversion of the criminal justice apparatus in Gujarat, and led to powerful intervention by the Supreme Court. The NHRC itself took the extremely unusual step of recommending to the Supreme Court that such major test cases be shifted to courts outside Gujarat, to ensure exemplary justice.

More recently, organizations like Jan Vikas established police venality in the Bilkis rape and massacre case, and forced the re-opening of investigations in a matter in which justice had been buried, and the men in khaki were severely indicted. Nineteen-year-old Bilkis Bano of Randikpur village, who was five-months pregnant at the time, was gangraped, and escaped being murdered by her assaulters only because she fell unconscious, and was assumed to be dead. She is the lone surviving witness to fourteen murders and eight gang rapes including her own. When she told her story to the police, they merely took her thumb impression on a blank sheet of paper and then registered an FIR which did not mention rape and referred only to violence by an unknown mob. The men she named walked away free, and the police characterized her as mentally 'unstable'. It was only after the intervention of human rights lawyers, that a medical examination was ordered, but since fifteen days had elapsed no evidence of rape was detected. The case stood closed as far as the police was concerned, and members of the force had even added salt to the dead bodies in the hope that no trace would be left of the decomposed corpses in their unmarked mass graves.

Over six years, this young and barely literate wife of a cattle trader stood her ground with extraordinary courage and resoluteness, surviving in hiding, continually on the move with her husband and child, born months after her violation, like fugitives, and succeeded eventually in bringing the guilty to justice. A special court in Mumbai sentenced eleven men to life imprisonment, and incarcerated a policeman for three years for trying to destroy evidence. Bilkis was bolstered by her husband Yakub's steady support, and the exemplary solidarity of human rights activists Gagan Sethi and Farah Naqvi. Bilkis herself has grown into a symbol for the entire nation of extraordinary courage in the face of enormous fear and adversity, and the sentence that she secured for those guilty of sexual violence in a communal pogrom is unparalleled in the legal system.

Away from the media spotlight, the Foundation for Civil Liberties has secured two extraordinary convictions, in the mass murders of Gharghoda and Anjanwada, and this too from courts within Gujarat. In the sombre hopeless climate of settled hate and mortal fear that has gripped large tracts of the Gujarati countryside, the victory of the residents of village Ghodasar is all the more inspiring. Unnoticed by the media, the humble villagers, mostly farm workers, secured from a police apparatus and lower judiciary, that is notoriously corroded with partisan communal prejudice, the first conviction of life imprisonment against twelve of their attackers. Stunningly, this came within just twenty months of the crime.

On that fateful day in 2002, mobs in their village attacked first their mosque, then their shops and homes. The villagers cowered in terror for two days and nights amidst the standing crops of the fields in the neighbouring village of Jalampur, whose residents gave them cover and protection. But on the third day, a mob of nearly 1500 people traced them. Fourteen people were killed, all elderly, including two seventy-year-old women. Investigations into their police complaint began desultorily six weeks after the tragedy, when they were still in makeshift relief camps. A delegation of village elders visited the survivors to say that if they wished to return to their village, they must refuse to give evidence to the police, and contradict their police complaint. A meeting of the village residents, however, resolved that they would not trade truth and justice even for the security of returning to their former homes.

Based on the statements, leading local Hindutva activists named in their complaints were arrested. As the matter reached the district court at Nadiad, alarm spread in the ranks of the attackers. A high level delegation, comprising senior Sangh and VHP leaders and lawyers, visited the villagers to negotiate. This time the inducement of money was added. The dispossessed villagers, mostly landless, had received less than Rs 10,000 each from the government for their destroyed homes and shops. But they resolutely refused to bow to both the threats and the bribes.

It is a testimonial to their steadfast courage and integrity even under such odds, that not one of forty-eight witnesses turned hostile or altered their statements in court. They were assisted by a dedicated team of human rights activists of the Foundation for Civil Liberties. The witnesses confidently identified the killers in the courts, and told the bench how the accused had slaughtered their loved ones and neighbours.

The life imprisonment given to twelve of the accused electrified the entire region. The Muslim residents of Ghodasar village returned to their homes, unhindered. Today they live in houses rebuilt by a relief organization, none threaten them and many have found jobs once again as farm workers. The pain and memories linger, but there is now no fear in their hearts.

A second category of legal cases spear-headed by human rights defenders relates to arrests and trials under the undemocratic anti-terrorism law, POTA, which has been used exclusively against minorities in Gujarat. There have been some acquittals and some convictions by the special court established to try the anti-terror matters, but there has been powerful defence by some of the finest legal talent of the country of the people incarcerated and charged under POTA.

The Jan Sangharsh Morcha led by activist Mukul Sinha is resolutely fighting for justice in another battlefield and relentlessly ensuring that truth is documented for posterity about state failures and crimes in 2002 and thereafter. There has also been enormous mobilization of survivors by the Jan Sangharsh Morcha, to testify before the Nanavati Shah Judicial Commission appointed by the state government to enquire into the 2002 communal violence. Regardless of allegations of bias, this is a very important forum where those who suffered unspeakable crimes can officially record the truth for posterity. It also collected clinching evidence to disprove conclusively the official statement of the state government and Hindutva organizations that the fatal fire on the train in Godhra on 27 February 2002, which fuelled the mass violence and pogrom against Muslims, was a terrorist conspiracy by Ghanchi Muslim people of Godhra; it was probably an accident.

Another category of legal action relates to the quest for a more just package of compensation, relief and rehabilitation. This has not only challenged the paltry and discriminatory norms that are established for compensation, relief and rehabilitation of the survivors, but also levied the charge that even these minimalist entitlements have been systematically withheld by a hostile and partisan state.

My own engagement, also with litigation in the Supreme Court, relates to more than 2000 cases that were closed after investigation without even trial, and nearly 300 cases which were heard in court with deliberately weakened and openly partisan investigation and prosecution. Not unsurprisingly, the accused were acquitted. This petition was undertaken with the assistance of leading human rights lawyer Indira Jaisingh of the Lawyers' Collective and Aman Biradari.[1]

Last but not least, there is Nyayagrah, a community-based, ethically bounded campaign for legal justice, which aims at approaching survivors with the assurance of support if they wish to fight for legal justice, and helps them contest these several hundred cases, mainly through the agency of the survivors, community justice workers and a number of young lawyers. I consider myself privileged to be a part of this movement.

Far from there being any inherent conflict between the efforts for reconciliation and legal justice, we believe that the only authentic reconciliation is one that is founded on justice. Any peace that is based on surrendering to fear and injustice is a counterfeit peace. It is not just peace and reconciliation that we seek. It is peace and reconciliation that is in itself just.

⚬

Especially in a democracy, in situations of persisting injustice, hate and fear, efforts for legal justice can powerfully help create conditions in which egalitarian spaces exist for estranged and divided people to renegotiate and forge bonds of mutual trust and amity. It can do this by shattering the aching and suffocating silences that are born out of dread and intimidation, by coercing out of this quietude an acknowledgement of the terrible and painful truths of what people have suffered in sectarian violence, and by establishing their equality before the Constitution and the law of the land, irrespective of the god they worship, their caste, gender and ethnicity. For the victims, it can challenge their resigned or sullen despair. For the perpetrators, it can deter further violence by convincing them of the legal consequences of their offences. For the people and organizations that manufacture disaffection and divide, it can break the norm of impunity that destroys the foundations of secular democracy.

It *can* do all of this. But efforts for, or even the eventual achievement of the ends, of legal justice need not necessarily facilitate egalitarian reconciliation. There is an even greater chance for striving for legal justice to achieve authentic reconciliation if the battle is actually fought by large numbers of the victims of mass hate violence themselves, and not remotely by lawyers and human rights agencies acting on their behalf. The chances of healing are even greater if local members of the community that meted out the violence are also encouraged to partner efforts for legal justice. The contest for legal justice should be bound by ethical rules in which the means deployed in the struggle are consistent with the ends of the battle. There must be vigilance and self-critical reflection at every stage of the struggle to ensure that the victim is never taken for granted. Every decision regarding the progress of the case must be taken with the informed consent of the victim survivor. And most importantly, the struggle should be based on truth, because untruthful or unjust means can never secure an authentically truthful and just set of outcomes.

Even such a mass people's campaign will not necessarily lead to reconciliation. But I believe that, without it, what is achieved is an unjust peace that may *look* like reconciliation to a detached outsider but, to those who live this counterfeit peace, it is only an abject surrender that daily shames and diminishes them. As Bilkis Bano declared after the court verdict sentencing the accused to life imprisonment, 'This judgment does not mean the end of hatred that I know still exists in the hearts and minds of many people . . . but it does mean that somewhere, somehow, justice can prevail.' She added aptly, 'This judgment is a victory not only for me but for all those innocent Muslims who were massacred and all those women whose bodies were violated only because, like me, they were Muslims.'

Communal pogroms such as the one that swept through Gujarat in 2002 pose grave threats to a robust, pulsing, functioning (though admittedly flawed) secular democracy in India. A democracy that is as much about the will of the majority as it is about the protection of the rights of minorities. The secular Constitution of India guarantees protection to all citizens to practise and propagate their faiths, and guarantees them equality before the law. It builds on age-old indigenous traditions of religious tolerance, pluralism and cultural accommodation.[2] But Modi's resounding victory in the state assembly elections barely months after the 2002 carnage, his continued unrepentant official hostility towards a section of people belonging to a minority faith throughout his tenure, and his return in 2007 with triumphant communalism barely disguised as an agenda for development, establishes as we noted formidable challenges to reconciliation. Siddhartha Vardharajan argues that Modi, the ruling party—in this case the BJP—and the fraternal organizations of the right-wing RSS, have succeeded in establishing a hierarchy of suffering; between that of the immediate victim community (the Muslims) and the allegedly long-suffering majority community of the Hindus.[3] This aims at creating a moral universe in which questions of official accountability and justice can be postponed indefinitely so that the manifest failure of the state to provide security to all is condoned.

Equally significant is the prevailing tradition of impunity that both state and communal organizations that foment and facilitate riots have enjoyed in most communal riots since Independence. Paul Brass, a social scientist who has devoted several decades of his life to studying communal riots in India, argues that even applying the term 'riot' to violence involving people and properties belonging to Hindus and Muslims in India is inappropriate, because it suggests images of a more or less spontaneous battle fought between people of varying and competing religious identities, whereas he observed that the mass violence 'was neither spontaneous, nor was it primarily conflict between Hindu and Muslim crowds'.[4] Brass writes, 'What are called Hindu–Muslim riots in India are, in fact, more like pogroms, and have recently, in Gujarat and elsewhere, taken the form of genocidal massacres and local ethnic cleansing as well'. This is made possible because of 'the complicity of the police and the failure of the political parties in control of government and the administrative and police officers in the districts to prevent riots or at least to contain them once they had begun'. He also documents in many of his works what he describes as 'institutionalised riot systems', and maintains that this 'was much more highly developed and elaborately organized within the network of militant Hindu organizations radiating out from the RSS than from any comparable network of Muslim organizations, at least in northern India'.[5]

As a district administrator for several decades, having both managed and observed riot situations closely, I fully endorse Brass's insights. Riots are rarely spontaneous; they are carefully planned and fostered on the sustained manufacture of hatred by dedicated and organized communal organizations. Further, he is accurate about state complicity in most riots, because I affirm that no communal violence can continue beyond even a few hours without the active concurrence of state and civil authorities. As I have observed earlier, the law adequately equips civil and police authorities who are present at the site of violence to take independent decisions regarding the application of force to control the mass violence, yet increasing numbers of officials choose to consult and comply with the partisan and unlawful will of their superiors and political leaders.

However, despite a convincing, some would say incontrovertible, body of evidence of assaults on the rights of the minority community, it is remarkably difficult to hold state authorities legally accountable for these denials, or to use the independent democratic institutions of state and civic action to punish them and actually end, let alone reverse, the extinction of citizens' rights.

The problem lies primarily in the fact that although the state *is* the principal duty-bearer for the enforcement of these rights and is enabled to act by the law and various statutes to defend these rights, it is not required to *compulsorily* act in such defence by the law. Second, the rights of the victims of such mass sectarian violence are largely implicit in the Constitution and statutes, but not explicitly and elaborately codified in the law, especially the mechanisms for the enforcement of these rights. And finally, the law and indeed the entire criminal justice system is constructed on the premise that the state will always best defend the rights of victimized individuals and social groups, therefore it does little to protect the rights of victims from the perverse actions of the state itself and its institutions.

There is no doubt that it was through individual, mostly non-state, actors who were directly responsible for the crimes that occurred in Gujarat, and indeed in innumerable prior incidents of communal violence occurred. And it has rightly been the concern of state institutions, survivors and human rights agencies to hold them legally accountable for these crimes. But there is also growing acknowledgement that the state too is vicariously responsible for the violation of human rights because its own acts of commission and omission enable the violence to unfold and it fails to protect the victims from these violations. The clearest statement that the responsibility for gross violation of human rights caused by communal violence is not merely that of the individual perpetrators of the crimes, but also of the state because of its failure or neglect to prevent the violations within its jurisdiction, comes from a landmark observation of the statutory NHRC.

Deeply disturbed by state failures after the mass communal violence of 2002, the NHRC stated that it had 'reached the definite conclusion that the principle of '*res ipsa loquitur*' applies in this case and that there was a comprehensive failure of the state to protect the Constitutional rights of the people of Gujarat'. It explains that the term 'res ipsa loquitur' means that the affair speaks for itself, or in other words the failures of the state are manifest in the events as admitted by the state government itself in its report of 12 April 2002 submitted to the commission. The NHRC held the state government responsible if it fails to rebut the presumption arising against it by explaining in a satisfactory and credible way that the mass violence occurred and could not be averted in spite of its efforts in the discharge of its constitutional duties. The commission gave the state government opportunity to explain, but ultimately concluded that it had failed to do so convincingly, and therefore it was indeed responsible for the grave denial of people's rights associated with the mass violence of 2002. It added that the state failed to discharge its 'primary and inescapable responsibility to protect the rights to life, liberty, equality and dignity of all of those who constitute it', and further elaborated the extremely important principle that the 'responsibility of the state extended not only to the acts of its own agents, but also to those of non-state players within its jurisdiction and to any action that may cause or facilitate the violation of human rights'.

In so doing, the NHRC was not creating a new jurisprudence: it was only reiterating—at the critical historic moment in which these rights stood most threatened and were being extinguished with impunity by the governments in Gujarat and Delhi—principles that have been upheld by many rulings of the high courts and Supreme Court of India. The courts have repeatedly affirmed that victims of communal and terrorist violence suffer not merely from the individual crimes to which they were subject, but also from the failure of the state to uphold their fundamental rights under the

Constitution, most importantly the fundamental right to life as guaranteed under article 21 of the Indian Constitution. For instance, in Bhajan Kaur vs Delhi Administration(1996), the Delhi high court held that such riots 'more often than not take place due to weakness, laxity and indifference of the administration in enforcing law and order.[6] If the authorities act in time and act effectively and efficiently, riots can surely be prevented.' Likewise in Manjit Singh (2005) it is observed that riots occur 'on account of laxity and indifference of the administration in enforcing law and order', and that these constitute a serious violation of the citizen's fundamental rights to life and equality before the law.

These principles have been reiterated in a large number of similar rulings related to injuries or deaths caused by state failures and negligence.[7] However, there are major problems in the current modes envisaged by courts for the enforceability of these rights. In most court rulings, the only recourse that is prescribed for making amends to citizens for failures of specific state actors is monetary compensation from the state exchequer to the victims. This is laudable in itself, but also ironic that while private individuals in similar circumstances are punishable with death and life imprisonment, state authorities who abet such crimes are not personally liable.

Also, though the law assigns powers to state authorities to protect the rights of all its citizens, what it does not contain is measures to require state authorities to use these powers in certain contingencies such as the outbreak or threat of outbreak of communal violence, with fairness and promptness, and to punish them if they deliberately fail to so act.

Whereas the failures as documented in the context of the Gujarat carnage 2002 are arguably the most grave and extensive in independent India, there is a great deal of evidence gathered by official commissions of enquiry that many of these failures have occurred in many previous communal riots, and that guilty state authorities have rarely, if ever, been punished for these lapses. Such impunity persists well beyond the failures to control violence, and extends, as in Gujarat, to refusals to provide security, relief and rehabilitation to the victims; and to the subversion of the criminal justice system which allows the perpetrators to escape punishment. These failures are so common that it is reasonable to assume that they recur at least in part because of the way the law at present is designed and interpreted by the courts.

There is no doubt that jurisprudence regarding the rights of survivors of communal riots to compensation marks the beginnings of a growing and welcome awareness about victims' rights. But my argument is that it does not go far enough. Those charged to protect the fundamental rights of citizens in the state should be individually liable for exemplary punishment for their failures that leave such a long trail of injustice and intense and avoidable human suffering. Also, it can no longer be presumed that the state will defend the rights of victims in all cases. The victim should also have rights, such as to adduce evidence in the trial courts even independently of the prosecution, and to file appeals against orders that acquit the accused. Victims, in practice, remain at the mercy of the state executive, or in some instances, the highest judiciary for the actual realization of these rights, and for recompense in the event of failure.

In the context of persisting impunity in a democratic polity, it is meaningless and misleading to focus efforts for reconciliation in Gujarat today exclusively on dialogues between the victims–survivors and the perpetrators of the crimes. No doubt they need to come together to find ways to fight the hate, fear and distrust that trap them all. But how can the affected people of Gujarat possibly look ahead with any confidence to a shared, peaceful and secure future, if those who manufacture, plan, execute and sustain campaigns of hate are untouched by both the law of the land and the promises of the secular democratic Constitution? How can they feel secure when officers who deliberately fail in their duties to protect all citizens regardless of their faith, caste or gender are not punished in any way, but are instead rewarded with flourishing careers?

The difficult and troubled path to reconciliation after violent ethnic conflict, particularly in the context of a secular democratic polity like India, *must* involve a challenge to the norm of impunity from the local to the highest levels. It must demonstrably redeem the constitutional promise of equality before the law of all citizens as a necessary, but admittedly insufficient, condition to bridge the gap between separated groups and heal old wounds. Justice must first be retributive—without being vengeful—and meted out fairly by state institutions of restored legitimacy, before it can be authentically restorative. Only then can both the victim and the perpetrator co-exist with a sense of shared protection.

11

From Satyagrah to Nyayagrah: Justice for Reconciliation and Healing

Apart from the norm of impunity, the striking feature of contemporary Gujarat after the massacre of 2002 which we observed are of frozen compassion and congealed hate and fear in social relations, the elaborate continuing subversion of justice, and the arrest of the processes of reconciliation.

Little has changed for the survivors of the Gujarat carnage of 2002, as they continue to negotiate survival amidst fear and hate, despite the passage of more than seven years and a major change of regime in New Delhi. Their myriad lacerations refuse to heal, as an unrepentant state government continues to subvert and destroy justice and all norms of civilized and humane governance. In the climate of fear and hostility, as well as economic and social boycott, which continues to prevail in many parts of Gujarat, many thousand survivors continue to languish without hope, security, homes and livelihoods. The government still refuses to reach out with resources and support to enable people to rebuild their lives. The survivors still face the widespread economic and social boycott and those who returned to their homelands live as second-class citizens, in submission and fear.

Reconciliation and healing are impossible from such a position of social surrender, humiliation and fear. For this reason above all, the battle for justice must be fought in the courts, judicial and human rights commissions, the Parliament and legislature. But most importantly of all, it has to be fought by the *people themselves*, in the places they live and work, and in their hearts and minds. This is a strike against manufactured fear and hate, a struggle for equal rights before the law, regardless of one's faith, caste, class or gender. It is a battle against forgetting.

❧

But for the possibility of reconciliation to be achieved through legal justice, what is important is not just that the end of justice under the law be accomplished; it is the means by which the struggle for legal justice is waged. Indeed, even if it transpires that the end of legal justice is not ultimately secured by mass, community-based and ethically bounded legal action, the process of mass non-violent democratic struggle for legal justice may itself beat a pathway that leads towards genuine, more egalitarian negotiations.

In the quest for appropriate means to achieve the ends of legal justice in ways that pave a pathway for authentic reconciliation, it was natural for us to look towards the theory and practice of one of the modern world's greatest and most resolute campaigners for justice, Mahatma Gandhi. He never tired of reminding those who fought along with him that in any struggle for peace and justice, it is imperative that the means deployed be fully compatible with its goals. Resistance for a more just, humane and genuinely democratic society cannot be built by means that are themselves unjust, inhuman and undemocratic. Brutal methods inevitably will produce brutalized outcomes. No amount of direct or structural violence justifies retaliatory violence. In the words of Martin Luther King Jr., 'Darkness can never drive out darkness. Only light can do that.' The idea that hate can only be conquered by love indeed has ancient roots. Buddha had said, 'Not by hate is hate defeated; hate is quenched by love. This is the eternal law.' The duty to resist injustice is also articulated in different ways by diverse traditions. Prophet Muhammad, for instance, prescribed, 'Whoever from amongst you sees an injustice, then he should rectify it using his hand, if he is unable to, then by his tongue, if he is unable to, then by his heart ... at least consider it to be a wrong'.[1]

Gandhi found the conviction for non-violent people's resistance for justice in an instrument which he termed 'satyagrah', or people's resistance for truth. He fashioned it as a mode of ethical, non-violent mass resistance against unjust laws and legal regimes. In 2006, we observed the passage of a century since the historic moment when Gandhi first started his satyagrah against the racist policies of the South African government. In his words, 'Civil disobedience becomes a sacred duty when the state becomes lawless or, which is the same thing, corrupt.' He believed that 'Non-cooperation and civil disobedience are different but branches of the same tree called Satyagraha.' It is important to note that in Gandhi's hands, civil disobedience was an intensely ethical tool: 'Disobedience to be civil has to be open and non-violent.' For him, it meant the 'capacity for unlimited suffering without the intoxicating excitement of killing ... Civil disobedience presupposes willing obedience of our self-imposed rules, and without it civil disobedience would be a cruel joke ... It implies discipline, thought, care, attention.'

Gandhi's use of satyagrah, or non-violent civil disobedience, against unjust laws in colonial and racist states inspired great later Gandhians like Martin Luther King Jr., who resisted racist laws and racial segregation in the United States, and like Nelson

Mandela and leaders of the African National Conference who struggled against apartheid in South Africa.

There are many inspiring examples of the use of satyagrah in contemporary Indian social movements, such as those for ecological democracy, gender, tribal and Dalit rights, rights to information, food and work, and labour rights. There are several unjust laws in India, such as those related to preventive detention, deployment of security forces against civilian populations, laws that criminalize begging and custodialize vulnerable groups; laws that compromise the rights of women and sexual minorities, and statutes for the compulsory acquisition of private lands, to name only a few. But at the same time, the statute books are strewn with progressive and just legislation that is rarely enforced, including for land reforms, the bans on bonded labour and untouchability, the outlawing of demeaning practices like carrying human waste on the head, restrictions on tribal land alienation and usurious money-lending, minimum wages, rights of inter-state migrants, the ban on dowry, the rights of survivors of domestic violence and entitlements of persons with disabilities. Often, the state violates its own progressive laws, and through that the rights of oppressed populations, with complete impunity. These many acts of omission result in insecurity, discrimination and on occasion grave mass violence against religious minorities, most dramatically in Gujarat, and this applies equally also to Dalits, women and tribal people in many parts of India. In formal democratic regimes where the laws frequently uphold justice, although in practice rights are openly violated in the mode of their implementation by state authorities, we are also confronted with a different mutation of lawlessness and wilful disobedience of just laws *not by the people but by the state*! And therefore, related but distinct instruments of democratic peaceful resistance from satyagrah need to be fashioned and widely deployed in these circumstances.

One such instrument of civic resistance that we propose is the idea we call 'Nyayagrah'—a people's campaign for legal justice and protection—for peaceful action to use the law and democratic instruments to secure justice. Satyagrah was a form of mass resistance to unjust laws. Nyayagrah—literally people's demand for justice—is proposed as mass campaigns not to disobey unjust laws, but instead to hold the state accountable to actually enforcing rather than disobeying its own just laws and to uphold rights guaranteed by the country's Constitution and laws and international covenants. It may involve access also to courts, but this is not mandatory because courts themselves may be part of the process by which rights are withheld and violated with impunity.

It is often assumed that there are mainly only two binary opposed options available to people who suffer from settled structural forms of injustice. One of these is to submit passively to the injustice, either with angry or humiliating resignation, or by making peace with it and possibly finding ways of individual escape, for oneself or one's family. Opposed to this is the possibility of violent resistance, through armed struggle, guerrilla warfare or terrorist violence. However, the admittedly still contested international regime of rights supported by laws and progressive Constitutions in many countries has greatly enlarged spaces for many forms of resolute people's peaceful resistance. These may be by forms of civil disobedience and non-cooperation in cases where laws and regimes are unjust and illegitimate, and by many forms of peaceful mobilization and legal activism for explicating rights and making them judiciable, and for making recalcitrant states accountable for the enforcement of just laws and the legal rights of oppressed women and men, boys and girls.

A small example of the practice of Nyayagrah is a people's campaign that strives for mass, community-based and ethically bounded legal justice for the survivors of the Gujarat massacre of 2002. The Nyayagrah campaign attempts—in response to the mass communal violence, impunity, subversion of the legal system and continued fear and hate—to mobilize the survivors to stand up in courts and name those who led the killings, rape, arson and looting in 2002. This is extremely difficult in a climate of intense settled fear, hate and boycott in which the minority community continues to survive more than seven years after the carnage. The battle is therefore less a legal battle, and more a contest against mass fear and hate, against endemic despair and surrender, and against imposed forgetting. It is based on the conviction that love is indeed possible after slaughter, but only with justice.

I wish to start this description with a disclaimer. When I recount some of the experiences and strivings of Nyayagrah, it is by no means my claim that there are no problems or major shortcomings or failings with our work, our organization and our philosophy. Far from it, we have found that we are not yet organized sufficiently to deal with the more than 240 cases that the victims have chosen to fight at the time of writing (and the numbers are likely to grow), and there are many unfortunate lapses and slips in courts. We have built a lot of trust and solidarity with the victim–survivors, but have not been equally successful in achieving the same with other human rights groups working in Gujarat, for a variety of reasons including the failings of our work. The consent of victims to fight the legal battle against their tormentors still wavers and on occasion even slips, because consent is given by victims in extremely difficult circumstances, of fear, intimidation and boycott. The consequences of boycott may be too hard to bear, or there may be pressures even from within one's community or even one's family. When we talk of our ethical rules, it is not our claim that our conduct measures up to the high standards that we have set ourselves. Adhering to the ethical rules of Nyayagrah is often a major struggle, and there remain recurring dilemmas and lapses. Although my colleagues in Gujarat have tried to maintain a very modest way of working, we continue to be dependent on external resources for our work. We agonise frequently, sometimes lose heart, and our optimism often ebbs and conviction falters but we continue to persevere despite many moments when we are unsteady and stumble.

With these disclaimers, the question we started with is: who should fight the battle for justice and reconciliation? The first article of faith of Nyayagrah is that this peaceful contest of peace must be led and waged by ordinary people themselves, especially people affected by the violent sectarian crimes, by people who are drawn from both sides of the embattled communities.

I firmly believe that if our country today remains secular and humane despite national and global mobilization around hate and difference, it is primarily because of its large mass of ordinary, working people, and the choices that they make even as they struggle and cope with the extremely difficult conditions of their lives. They defend secularism, justice, humanism and democracy, and indeed the idea of India itself, in myriad different ways—in their politics and social objectives; in the manner they choose to live their lives; in the ways they earn their living and spend their money; in what they teach their children and speak of to their friends; in the dreams of young people and the wisdom of the old; in their worship and in their irreverence; in the songs they sing, the books they read, and the films they choose to watch; in their solidarities and friendships; in those they choose to align with and those they choose to fight; in their spoken voices and in their eloquent silences; in multi-hued ways of shared living crafted over millennia.

It is for this reason firstly that in Nyayagrah we proposed to work primarily with 'ordinary' working people—recognizing them to be our greatest resource and strength.

From the start of the pogrom seven years ago, I observed how the parched humanity of Gujarat was moistened most by the ordinary people of our land, by the stream of volunteers, mostly young people, who poured into Gujarat, eager to contribute in whatever way they could, to show that they cared, and to suffer with their fellow citizens in Gujarat. For many, it was an act of penance, for others a pilgrimage of caring. Many more sent donations, from wage workers in Lucknow to rich industrialists in Mumbai.

I recall a team of auto-rickshaw drivers who arrived from Andhra Pradesh, led by young Saddam Basha, who lived in camps in Ahmedabad for over three weeks at a time, cheerfully sacrificing their daily earnings back home. Of all the volunteers, they were perhaps the most loved. Women in the camps blessed them and declared that they had been more to them than their sons. They wept when the young men finally returned to their homes. I remember an unlikely band of youthful executives working with multi-national companies in Mumbai, who were so moved by the carnage that they would every weekend put away their suits and travel to Ahmedabad to serve in the camps. A village volunteer from the Mazdoor Kisan Shakti Sangathan in Rajasthan visited a camp and observed that the toilets were intolerably dirty, choked with excreta and had not been cleaned for days. Unmindful of the nauseating stench and strict caste taboos, without a word, he set about cleaning the toilets for several hours. When he returned the next morning, residents of the camp surrounded the toilets, refusing to let him enter. They had resolved to take up the duty from then on themselves.

I was most touched by the peace and justice volunteers— whom we called aman and nyaya pathiks, those who walk the path of peace and justice—many of them young men and women who responded to our call in Ahmedabad. Several of the volunteers having themselves suffered gravely in the carnage, I wondered how many of us in their position would be able to summon the same inner resources to forgive so quickly and help others in need.

The 'frozen compassion' of Gujarat was thawed by hundreds of Hindus who saved the lives of their Muslim neighbours. In the hour of national darkness, many lamps of compassion, humanity and courage were lit with resolution and faith by our ordinary people. With quiet individual acts of caring and courage, it is not the state, not organized civic action, but the spontaneous acts of individual people, in Gujarat and in several corners of the country, which defended the gravely threatened humanism and democratic traditions of our land. As we stumble deep into the dark night in this defining moment in our collective history, if the agony of our land heals and the rivers of poison dry up, if love and tolerance are restored to our public life, it will be because of our 'ordinary' people. It is ultimately because of them that we are still able to hope amidst the darkness of Gujarat.

Our conviction that battles for legal justice should be fought by people drawn from the communities that are torn apart by hate stems from the fact that despite the manufactured and organized campaigns of hate in Gujarat, there are innumerable acts of individual resistance, extraordinary compassion and courage by ordinary people. I have spent—both physically and emotionally—many moments of my life in the seven years since the carnage in the affected regions of Gujarat, and encountered so many stories of kindness at every turn, that I now estimate that for every act of brutality and cruelty, there are at least two or three of kindness. This is the untold story of the Gujarat massacre and, I suspect, of all previous communal pogroms and riots as well. Much more than the middle classes, it is 'ordinary' people who have held on to their essential humanity, often at great personal risk.

This is not a random romantic idealistic observation. Ashis Nandy, part of a large cross-country study into Partition memories, speaks of 'another kind of forgetting', not 'an obsessive, private engagement with memories—stealthy, compulsive returns to the past to refresh paranoia and self-destructive fantasies of revenge'.[2] Instead, he finds himself at last able to mourn the death of more than a million people during the Partition, because '26 per cent of the respondents in our survey say that they survived because of help given by someone from the enemy community'. He rightly describes this as grass-roots resistance to genocide, pointing out that 'No other genocide in the world yields comparable figures. And even that figure is an underestimation. Many victims are loath to admit that they have survived because someone from the enemy community helped.' Nandy describes a moving story recorded by his research collaborator from the other side of the border, Salim Ahmed of Islamabad's Sustainable Development Policy Institute, of how 'an elderly Sikh was disturbed when his son brought home an abducted Muslim woman; he begged his son to release the woman. But the son was young and women were being abducted all over Punjab. He did not listen. The father took out his gun and shot his son.' This story was recounted to him by a member of the woman's family, and Salim has already found more than a hundred such episodes ...

❧

Our further conviction is that the battle for legal justice is not an end in itself. It is primarily an instrument for the victim to re-establish her or his equal citizenship and rights before the law in a secular democracy. And if she chooses to fight it, then we must build adequate community-based systems of support and solidarity to aid her battle. The contest for legal justice must assist the victim battle the fear and dread in her heart, and the hate in the heart of her neighbour. For the criminal case to impact the victim's own diminished sense of citizenship and humanity, the decision of whether and how to fight the battle can and must be primarily that of the victim. It must be she who takes informed and binding decisions about the case, and not the best-motivated and qualified lawyers and human rights activists who support her.

Most often, struggles for justice using the law are fought by lawyers and human rights defenders *for* the victim, in her name and on her behalf. It is reasonably believed that the victim, after all, cannot be expected to understand the complexities of the legal system, and even less the ways to negotiate its opaque treatises to secure ultimate legal victory. Therefore, the victims are rarely consulted about important decisions regarding the case, and professional and well-meaning human rights workers sometimes neglect to inform these survivors even about the way the case is progressing. Their existence is recalled only when they have to give evidence in court, for which they have to be suitably 'prepared' if the case is to be 'won', or occasionally by alert human rights defenders if they report being threatened so as to plead for witness protection. They are demonized if they turn 'hostile' in court or succumb to intimidation or inducement to change their statements. It is ironical that the victim is almost instrumentalized for the 'larger' purpose of a greater justice. This is a grave danger when large and high profile cases of major and spectacular massacres, involving significant numbers, are taken up as symbolic 'test cases' to uphold the rule of law. The 'weak' witness who succumbs to intimidation or inducement, or both, is seen to fail not just his own case, but the entire victim community and indeed the lofty cause of justice itself. I do not believe any victim—even one who prevaricates, surrenders, or submits to inducements or intimidation—should be made to carry burdens of stigma greater than those he or she already bears.

We have already referred to the outstanding efforts of some human rights organizations who have taken up a few such 'major' criminal cases of the Gujarat carnage of 2002, and this strategy has unarguably significantly advanced the cause of justice in the country in ways never achieved in the aftermath of earlier mass communal violence. They have employed the best legal talent to fight these cases, spent significant resources to support the witnesses through the trials, and the strong verdicts given by the Supreme Court, coupled with widespread media attention to these matters, has resulted in salutary outcomes to challenge impunity and subversion of justice well beyond those specific incidents, victims and perpetrators.

They have together covered more than 10 per cent of the cases that were registered at that time. This is a large number. But at the same time, another incontestable aspect of the realities for the survivor is that 90 per cent of the cases, mainly those deemed in objective terms of the scale of loss of life, limb and property, to be 'smaller' cases, are left to their own devices, and many are reduced to haplessly trading their return to their homeland and safety for pursuit of legal justice. Criminal cases are collapsing repeatedly because witnesses are too frightened to speak the truth, although their fearful silences may diminish them each day in their *own* eyes.

To complement the magnificent and courageous efforts of organizations that are pursuing a select number of test cases, we adopted a strategy of mass prosecution of as many of these 'small cases' as the affected people themselves choose to fight (at very modest costs) through Nyayagrah. It is an attempt to be available to extend legal and moral support to any survivor who wishes to engage in mass prosecution despite the personal costs and risks that it entails for them. We feel also that transacting a large number of cases decreases the risks of those represented individuals facing harassment and police oppression. Although pursuing mass prosecution means that not all cases may achieve success, it puts enormous pressure on the system, forcing the police and the courts to respond. Nyayagrah decided to try to reach out to every single victim in the districts of Gujarat that we chose for our work— Ahmedabad, Gandhinagar, Anand, Kheda and Sabarkantha (these five districts together incidentally account for around 60 per cent of all criminal matters registered after the 2002 carnage). For us, every single case is important if the victim regards it to be so, and wants to fight it through the legal system.

The first decision in any case of sectarian violence is of course the most critical one, of whether the victims and witnesses want to fight the case at all. For them to choose to fight is to resolve to publicly name their neighbours who persecuted them and their loved ones. The consequences of the decision can be very grave for the survivors: it can be intimidation, verbal, physical and sexual violence, further boycott, expulsion from the village, or entangling them in false counter-cases. The choice of whether to fight or not must therefore be the informed and empowered resolve of those who will have to actually face the consequences of the decision.

We therefore contact every survivor and witness, and try to reassure them of our steadfast emotional and legal support to the very end if indeed they choose to fight their cases in the police stations and courts. But we consciously offer them no financial support. We believe that people who live in such unequal circumstances should not be induced even subtly to choose to battle for legal justice. We do not have large resources to assist victims with livelihoods and house-building or educational support for their children, but we assure them that whatever assistance we do offer will not be influenced by their choice whether to fight in courts, but by their need and our limited capacities. We also pledge our understanding and unconditional solidarity and continued friendship even if they elect *not* to fight, because we have no right to be judgemental about their choices in extremely difficult circumstances.

Once the survivor decides to fight the legal case, Nyayagrahis or justice workers ensure the legal literacy of every victim and witness so that they can be a part of the fight for justice.

Nyayagrah is, thus, a community based campaign, because it relies mostly on community justice workers, or nyaya pathiks, drawn from the affected communities, working-class young women and men, often themselves survivors, who volunteer to work for peace and justice, and are trained in the basics of law. These community justice workers try to help the survivors to rise above the hate and fear that has bitterly divided their communities and almost broken their spirits. They work without compromise, hate or fear with steadfast commitment to justice, and with compassionate and unfailing support for the survivors and witnesses. The broad duties of a nyaya pathik are to assist survivors of mass communal violence to overcome hate and fear, and to fight for legal justice in accordance with the victim's aspirations. They are trained to treat the victims and witnesses with great empathy and respect. They assure the victims of solidarity and support regardless of whether or not they choose to fight the legal cases; and in no circumstances to judge the victim or witness should they decide to compromise or not fight, remembering they are coping as best as they can with very difficult circumstances. Apart from collecting information about various aspects of the cases, understanding and explaining to the victims what stage the case has reached, they are also charged with assisting vulnerable survivors of mass communal violence, especially widows, children and unsupported old people, to rebuild their livelihood and shelters in accordance with their aspirations.

Their ultimate duty is to promote processes of genuine and egalitarian reconciliation and healing in the communities that were torn apart by the mass violence and hate mobilization, including where possible to facilitate the dignified return of people to their homes.

We have deliberately avoided labelling them 'paralegals', as this suggests a subordinate status—of less valued knowledge and skills—to lawyers. Instead, we constantly stress that although the community justice workers may have less formal education than the formally trained lawyers, they are fully equal partners of Nyayagrah. This is because Nyayagrah is basically a struggle against fear and hate, to be fought no doubt in police stations and courts, but also in homes and in farms, in factories and the streets, and above all in hearts and minds. Just as the lawyer is a specialist in law, the justice worker is a specialist in social processes, and Nyayagrah cannot achieve its objectives without either the lawyer toiling in courts, or the justice worker in the homes of victims. Justice workers are in leadership positions in Nyayagrah, and lawyers may report to people who may have less formal education but who distinguish themselves with sterling qualities of character. They are joined in this enterprise by young lawyers mostly fresh out of college who act as 'justice agents'.

My personal bonds with many of these young people began with my days and nights spent in the relief camps set up by the Muslim community in 2002 to shelter teeming numbers of internally displaced and intensely traumatised women, men and children. These days and nights that I spent with literally thousands of critically bereaved and dispossessed survivors living with stoic dignity in cramped and grossly under-resourced camps laid the foundations of our bonds for future solidarity. I made appeals in these camps for peace and justice volunteers or 'aman pathiks', and have worked closely with several of them for these many years.

One of the most painful journeys of my life, exactly six months after the massacre, was a trek of less than a kilometre, in the bylanes of Naroda, witness to some of the most brutal bloodshed in the history of Ahmedabad. With me were several aman pathiks, young people who had volunteered to serve and heal in response to our call after the carnage. Following the forced closure of Shah-e-Alam camp a few days earlier, refugees had been coerced to return with their families to what remained of their homes in this settlement of dread. Some slept in a cramped madrassa, others with relatives. As we slowly walked the narrow lanes, they pointed to the remains of their homes. Row after row of charred houses, collapsed masonry, cracked walls, open skies, burnt heaps, all crowded with aching memories and burnt earnings of many lifetimes. They recreated for us the ghoulish events, the murders, burning, rape, the terror, the escape, and the ones who could not get away. As we walked, our eyes repeatedly clouded and our shoulders stooped. I realized then, as I do each day I work with them, how much they had suffered and still they are able to find places in their hearts for forgiveness, and to work for peace and non-violent justice. I wondered if in their place I would have located the same spaces in my own heart.

I have learnt from each the enormity of their loss, sometimes accumulated over generations of communal riots, of homes repeatedly burnt down and looted, of the brutal loss or sexual violation of loved ones, of recurring uprootment, of retrenchment and boycott due to their minority faith, of interrupted schooling and childhood, of shame and anger and helplessness. Usman Shaikh was one among a few hundred young women and men who volunteered to work as aman pathiks and later as nyaya pathiks in the wake of the blood-drenched carnage of the spring of 2002 in Gujarat. Uprooted from his native Ahmedabad, Usman tirelessly shuttles between the ravaged and traumatized villages of rural Gujarat allocated to his charge. Together with other community workers and young lawyers, he strives to rebuild the brutally ruptured bonds of trust and harmony between the two profoundly estranged communities, to fight fear and hate, and uphold justice. I asked him once whether he missed his family in the long weeks that he is separated from them every month. He replied, 'Since 1969, my home has been looted and destroyed five times in communal riots. I am working so that it is not destroyed a sixth time.'

Most of the peace and justice workers are working-class people: drivers, conductors, electricians, embroiders, tailors, artisans, welders. They have found extraordinary resolve to forgive and work for peace. I have been frequently moved and humbled by their generosity. There are fewer but still significant numbers from the local Hindu community, including many Dalits, who have volunteered in the struggle for justice in which members of their own community are the perpetrators, and they daily brave taunts and rejection by members of their own community for 'siding with the enemy', but quietly persevere because of their commitment to justice and their personal vision of a shared humanity.

I recall Yusuf, Sharief and Imran, dispossessed young men who lost their homes to the fires of Naroda, whom I met in the relief camp in Shah Alam Dargah in Ahmedabad, whose resolve to work for justice and peace has not wavered through the vicissitudes of seven years of penury in their families. Yusuf was even implicated in a false case and spent four months with his father in Sabarmati Jail. I worried how this new trauma of injustice would embitter him, but it did not shake his resolve in any way. 'When I would be depressed in prison, my father would ask me to remember who else had been confined to the Sabarmati Jail. It was Gandhiji. "If Gandhiji could stay here, who are you and I?"' the ageing bus driver comforted his son Yusuf.

Sharief's eyes well over briefly as he recalls the tribulations of his family while starting life afresh after they lost their home and loved ones in the massacre of 2002 in Naroda Patia in Ahmedabad. 'If there is one man who is most responsible for our recovery, it is the owner of the factory in which my father works. Right from the months that we were at the relief camp, the Hindu *seth* ensured that my father got his salary every month. He kept his factory job vacant, and took him back as soon as we moved out from the camp, unlike thousands of other Muslims who were retrenched. He loaned us the money to rebuild our home, and said, "Don't bother if you cannot repay."' Sharief affirms with conviction, 'This is not a battle between Hindus and Muslims. It never was. It is only politics'.

Usman Shaikh finds it hard to listen day in and day out to the testimonies of the unrelieved suffering of the survivors, because their pain often reflects one's own. He adds that the work has changed him fundamentally. 'In earlier riots, I would not hesitate to join a mob and throw stones at one's attackers. But today all that I can think of is how to build peace'. He often laughs that one of the Hindu nyaya pathiks, Jaswant, lives in the colony just across his own, and they must have thrown stones at each other in past riots. Today he wonders at the miracle that they are working together for justice and peace.

There are many among them who show a remarkable aptitude for criminal law. Trained lawyers say that there is much that they learn about criminal law from an electrician like Nasir. Khalida studied till class five, but she constantly surprises both lawyers and victims with her legal acumen and instincts. The other Khalida, the oldest nyaya pathik, is a grandmother and barely literate, but there are few as skilled as her in building the morale of the survivors. Older widows like Afroz Apa battle their own demons of loneliness and bouts of clinical depression to fight for the rights of other widows—

both Muslim and Hindu—struggling at the same time to master the opaque complexities of law.

For Hindu justice workers like Bhanu Bhai, Kishore, Satish, Sadhubhai and Prakash, a quiet conviction about the righteousness of their battles carries them through customary taunts from friends and relatives about their treachery to their own communities. Dalit nyaya pathik Jaswant countered to an upper-caste acquaintance, who offered to find him alternative employment if he left Nyayagrah work, by asking, 'Tell me, would you then also invite me to your house, and eat with me?' Manibhai, a Dalit lawyer from an impoverished farming household in rural Anand who fought the cases of the Muslim survivors of the carnage even before Nyayagrah started work, has no regrets that many Hindu clients mock him for what they interpret to be his 'Muslim sympathies', even when they refuse to give him their briefs. 'Look, "2002" has come,' they jeer whenever he enters the courtroom. Jitendra Sahu is even more ostracized by his colleagues in the bench because he is a Brahmin. His Nyayagrahi colleagues remark often about his courage when he fearlessly confronts policemen in police stations, with the anger and passion of a personal battle. Everyone was surprised by the unsuspected reservoirs of courage that diminutive and unassuming young local lawyer Chiragbhai demonstrated when he spiritedly complained against a judge in Belol court, who openly displayed bias against the survivors by encouraging an out-of-court settlement in the case of a brutal murder. It was a case which many senior lawyers were unwilling to argue for fear of antagonizing the entire judicial system.

Prita Jha, a trained solicitor who grew up in the United Kingdom, chose, to the consternation and outrage of her parents, to shift to Ahmedabad with the pledge to partner the battle for legal justice for as long as it takes. 'I have often suffered from racism as I grew up in the UK,' she says, 'and I always believed that it was primarily the duty of the majority to defend the rights of minorities. Therefore when Gujarat happened, I felt that here I was from the majority community, therefore it was my turn to fight for the rights of the persecuted minority.' Johanna Lokhande grew up in Vadodara and has an outspoken sense of justice that drew her to Nyayagrah, and she remains a fierce critic of what she sees as humbug both outside and within Nyayagrah's battles for justice and the defence of secular democracy. Mushtaque Ali and Hanif ur Rahman trained in law in the Aligarh Muslim University. Their parents were also understandably worried by the risks for a young Muslim fighting for legal justice in Gujarat, with hardly any monetary recompense. Today they are proud of them. The two young lawyers chose to live in a relief colony near Anand, to demonstrate and actually live their solidarities with the survivors, and on this foundation many survivors built their trust of these fine young men.

Many senior lawyers were (and continue to be) highly sceptical about a legal battle of this completely unprecedented scale and magnitude (in the context of communal riots in India) being fought by what they justifiably perceive to be a motley bunch of community workers and admittedly idealistic but inexperienced lawyers mostly fresh out of the classroom. It seems to them a futile and foolhardy attempt to confront a modern army with a small band of villagers armed only with bows and arrows, and perhaps they are right. But this motley group has succeeded in reviving more than 200 cases so far, and the numbers are likely to grow. We believe that a battle of this kind requires integrity and courage, and not just professional legal acumen (although the latter is no doubt helpful). Law can be learned, but not character.

Every profession has tended to bitterly resist when it is confronted with attempts to demystify and democratize it by sharing its privileged knowledge with 'barefoot' lay people. This happened when community health workers challenged the monopoly of medical practitioners, and were attacked as dangerous quacks. Today they are widely acknowledged to have helped people gain control over their own health: restoring 'people's health in people's hands'. The same was the response to lay counsellors from professional psychiatrists, and barefoot engineers from the engineering community.

Like satyagrah, Nyayagrah tries also to draw up its ethical rules, and the Nyayagrahis strive to live up to these rules each of which has been passionately debated by the Nyayagrah team The ethical principle that has attracted the most searching challenge from members of the team is the resolve never to pay even a rupee as bribe at any stage of the legal process. Many have argued that this is an utterly impractical way of binding of our hands in what is an unequal fight, because even in normal circumstances, it is impossible to extract a copy of a legal document without bribing officials. The justice workers and lawyers cannot even begin to assist the victims at the stage of police investigation without copies of the police complaint or FIR and the panchnama; likewise the watching counsel of the victim when the case is taken to trial is helpless without copies of the charge-sheet, statements and court proceedings. These difficulties are compounded several times over when the state itself, and a majority of the police functionaries and several magistrates, are openly biased. These substantial barriers are further fortified when many of the justice workers are young, working-class Muslim men and women.

I recall an evening when a deeply frustrated justice worker telephoned me, reporting that in a crucial case, where court statements were to begin the next morning, the court clerk had demanded Rs 600 for copies of the relevant court papers. Without these documents, it was impossible to prepare the witnesses for their statements. The justice worker wanted to make an exception just once and pay the clerk the bribe that he demanded. I demurred, reminding him about our consensus to never pay a bribe irrespective of the circumstances, and he was furious. The statements, as it turned out, went well, based on our standard legal advice: *sach bolo, saaf bolo* (speak the truth, and speak it clearly). However, the disputation was carried over to our next review meeting, and after several memorable hours of debate and philosophical dialectics among my colleagues who had learned to differentiate between right and wrong not from books but from life, the principle that we cannot fight for truth by untruth was emphatically affirmed by almost all, including the nyaya pathik who had initially wanted to pay the bribe.

Today, in hindsight, most justice workers are happy that they follow this rule. It confirms in their own eyes the righteousness of their arduous battle for justice through 'right' means. But even at a practical level, they report that their stubborn refusal to pay bribes for papers from the police, combined with their courteous persistence, have contributed to gradual but radical changes in the attitudes of many police personnel. Earlier, the young working-class justice workers were rudely turned away when they asked for the papers in police stations, often with open or veiled threats. Today they testify that they are usually offered a seat, and tea, along with the papers. There are occasions that I have witnessed when the policemen have personally delivered the papers at the Nyayagrah office. They also report a change in the body language of many police personnel, from one of undisguised hostility to a grudging respect, and even possibly (I would like to believe) an unstated acknowledgement that they are fighting a just and brave battle.

There has been far greater ready acceptance of the other rule that also challenges 'common sense' practices of the legal profession, that all evidence will be based strictly on truth, with no construction of evidence. This makes legal advice to witnesses very simple and stark: '*sach bolo, saaf bolo!*' That involves making sure that they name the accused and the witnesses and they recount the actual events as they saw them without confusion. But the fact is that in many cases, they fled before the crimes were committed, such as of arson and looting of their properties. They have learnt the names of their tormentors second hand, and lawyers may have in other circumstances advised them to claim to be eye witnesses, to secure conviction. But this is ruled out by the stsndards that Nyayagrah has set for itself. Many lawyer friends are sceptical, even amused about these two rules. They ask the Nyayagrahis pertinently, 'Shouldn't winning the case be your biggest and only goal? Are you not trying to get a conviction, and send the accused to jail? Then why should you tie up your hands in ways that make winning even more difficult?' To this, the Nyayagrahis smile and say, 'Of course we fight to win. But even more important than winning the fight is *how* we fight.'

These principles of truth are carefully explained to the victims and witnesses, and again contrary to conventional expectations, these rules have tended to draw many more survivors to Nyayagrah than drive them away. In cramped segregated Muslim ghettoes, amidst frolicking children and goat kids, we explain to an attentive gathering the philosophy and objectives of Nyayagrah The nyaya pathiks explain that what they want is only an assurance of steadfast uncompromising adherence to truth, at every stage of the evidence. We have found consistently, especially in rural gatherings, that this ethically illuminated discourse, presented in homespun and direct language by the young justice workers, far from discouraging them, instead consistently energizes the community of victim–survivors, particularly women and the youth. It tends to draw them into bonds of warm and enduring solidarities with the Nyayagrah team, much more robust than any offer of financial support and more credible assurances of eventual legal victory by any means could, I like to think, possibly achieve.

ᴄ❧

Conventional wisdom regarding Nyayagrah was that legal justice was *our* agenda, as human rights workers, not that of the dispossessed victims, who were forced to negotiate daily survival and safety in a climate of continued insecurity and hate. The actual experience has been different. In a campaign of around two years at the time of writing, we have approached survivors involved in over 1263 criminal cases registered after the 2002 carnage in the five districts. Despite the prevailing pervasive fear and boycott, and the conditionality of not pursuing legal cases with the police and courts if they are to be allowed by the majority community to live and work in the lands of their ancestors, survivors in 240 of these cases, picked up extraordinary courage to pursue legal justice, ignoring the cost to their security and livelihoods. Since each case involves numerous incidents in a single village, this means that many more than 2000 survivors have chosen to stake their lives and futures, despite grave threats, to the pursuit of legal justice. They have also resisted inducements of cash that the now beleaguered accused are offering them to buy their silences.

When we set out in our work, we had no idea of the extent to which the survivors would choose to fight for legal justice. Despite formidable barriers, one in six witnesses has given us consent to fight her legal battles for justice through these same discredited courts and police stations whose doors seem barred to the poor and minorities. It has been our experience that the wealthier victims, such as shopkeepers and traders whose financial losses are large, tend to be much less willing to fight than poor working people, and women tend to display much more courage than men. There have been many meetings of victims in which women have shamed the men worried about the consequences to their security of legal battles against their neighbours into consent. Often, even the local Muslim community threatens boycott if people fight legal cases, because it destroys the fragile unequal peace that they have brokered. It is important to carefully hear the survivors about the importance of justice for them.

In one remarkable matter, a middle-aged Niyaz Bibi of Ongej village in Ahmedabad district even defied the decision of her husband and brothers-in-law and stood in court to name those who had destroyed their home, resulting in twelve arrests. Niyaz Bibi, who now lives in Juhapara relief colony, cannot forgive the attackers who caused her exile from her village, and she chose to fight her case, although even her own husband had consented to an unequal 'compromise' that bought their silence for some money and the 'permission' to sell their lands in the village at remunerative prices. '*Hamein ghar se bewatan kar diya unhon ne* (They exiled us from our homeland),' she says, heartbroken in her one-room tenement. '*Jo sach hai, so sach hai, bas* (What is the truth, is the truth!),' she declares passionately. When we question her about being frightened, she answers simply, '*Dar to mere bas ki baat hi nahi hai* (I find myself incapable of fear).' Many of the rioters who looted and destroyed their home and drove them out of the village were her children's friends. She had 'fed them when they were hungry ... How can I now forgive them? I want justice. I will fight for it till my last breath.' Not many have her strength to stand upright while confronting so many battles waged together.

Aayesha Ben, a widow of village Kishangarh in Sabarkantha district, still asks, 'What had I done to them? Why did they do this to me?' Hiding in a pit, she saw her shop being looted and burnt. She saw each person who was looting the shop yet in the FIR the police recorded, as it did all across burning Gujarat, only that the attack was by 'an unknown mob'. Aayesha Ben got her case reopened. Thirteen of the accused from her village were jailed for a week—a huge achievement in Gujarat. Each day she is threatened to take her case back but, determined to get justice, she refuses to give up. 'I want justice. I deserve it, don't I?' she asks simply.[3]

What spurs their search for justice? Is it only retribution, a longing for revenge? There is no doubt that this is frequently a part of the motivation. But most of all, it is a desperate search for acknowledgement. The survivors do not believe that their tormentors will ultimately be punished in the majority of cases, because even in normal times the legal system is heavily weighted against the poor. Simply the arrest of those who attacked them and looted and destroyed their homes, and their summoning to the police station and courts, satisfies them enormously, because it establishes to them and those who occupy their world that despite the deafening denials that surround them, they did indeed suffer unspeakable atrocities, often at the hands of their neighbours. It forces out a form of acknowledgement even from the jaws of the stubborn and powerful denial of the state and people of Gujarat. It establishes them as human beings and citizens who are equal before the law. I recall one victim who said, 'I do not expect to win the case. But so many years later, all I want is to ask my tormentors on at least three different occasions, "Where are you going?" and hear them reply despondently, "To the police station". Or, "to the courts". *Bas*, this is all I want. Let me hear this three times, and it will be enough to still the fires which continue to rage in my heart.'

Nyayagrahi Ishak Arab says that what people have suffered leaves a knot in their hearts. 'If they do not untie that knot, it can lead to many unfortunate outcomes later like violence.' Abdul Bhai, a shopkeeper of village Bharkad in Anand district, witnessed the loot, arson and destruction of the Muslim houses that took place in Bharkad. Yet, the police did not record his statement. It was many years later that Abdul Bhai managed to get his statement recorded and the case reopened. By then three of the accused had fled from India. Abdul Bhai has since received threats and has also got offers for compromise. He is under heavy debt but he is not giving up—there is no trade-off between justice and money. 'It's never been about money. It is about my self-respect. I want justice. If I let them get away this time it will happen again and again.'[4]

They also see in these efforts deterrence, that only if those who attacked them and their properties are forced to face the institutions and processes of criminal justice in this land, whatever the eventual outcomes, they may hesitate to take up arms against their neighbours the next time round. Many report with satisfaction that for the first time, many of their tormentors of the past now regret their acts during the carnage, because it drags them to courts, police stations and even jail. It forces a kind of remorse, even if it is motivated more by dismay at the adverse consequences for them than ethical regret. Stories such as of Lambadia village in Sabarkantha are also frequently recounted where, in an earlier riot, victims had fought for justice, leading to the imprisonment of their neighbours. As a consequence, in 2002, these same persons who had returned from jail rushed to protect their erstwhile victims because they feared that they would otherwise be charged if they were assaulted or robbed, regardless of their innocence.

Many are inspired by the outcomes of pursuing justice for the dignity, self-esteem and even the security of the victims, such as in Ghodasar village in Kheda, where victims, mostly farm workers, secured the first conviction in Gujarat after the

2002 carnage, of life imprisonment against twelve of their attackers within just twenty months of the crime. It is an unsung story of the greatest courage of humble survivors who refused to be cowed down, to surrender, be purchased, or break in extremely difficult circumstances. The pain and memories linger, but there is now no fear in their hearts.

೪

It is such forlorn but brave hopes of trampled survivors that most motivate their heroic fight for legal justice. Nyayagrah is only one small example of a people's fight for justice using democratic and legal instruments, combined with the survivors' own courageous resolve to peacefully fight injustice in solidarity with justice agents, among many that have been witnessed in independent India for upholding rights of the oppressed that are guaranteed by law but withheld by states acting with customary impunity.

A large number of factors will determine the degree to which the survivors will ultimately secure justice. To the extent that they do, they will contribute both to healing the wounds of the survivors and preventing the recurrence of such mass crimes with state complicity in future. In the words of leading human rights activist Girish Patel, this battle is not primarily about winning or losing, although we do hope to win the cases. 'It is far more importantly a crushed people's resolve to resist efforts by the state to exile them from the legal process itself, to deny them their rights as equal citizens of this country to access the legal system, with all its strengths and flaws. To the extent that even the efforts ultimately fail, they will constitute a significant people's resistance to injustice.'

It is by no means our claim that even if they are successful, efforts for legal justice fashioned authentically around the principles and strategies of Nyayagrah can in themselves lead to reconciliation. At best it can challenge the humiliating and inequitable surrender and capitulation that is forced on survivors who live in times of fear, hate and frozen compassion, and establish their equality before the law.

These remarkable heroic strivings for justice amidst fear, combined with myriad unsung, unacknowledged individual acts of compassion by women and men from different sides of the estranged people in times of hate, lay the strongest foundations for negotiating a peaceful and just shared future. Their iridescent acts of courage and humanity constitute the most powerful individual resistance to the politics of manufactured hate. They are the countless fireflies that combat the darkness of contemporary Gujarat and illuminate all our pathways in these deeply troubled times.

Epilogue:
Love in the Times of Fear and Hate

Like the sites of all great catastrophes and suffering, Gujarat abounds with thousands of untold stories. But not all are tales of massacres, hate, fear, despair and mass graves, of blood congealed on streets and poison in hearts. The stories much less recounted are those of most extraordinary human compassion and courage. For every narrative of cruelty and oppression that people recount of those tempestuous days of 2002, there are at least two or three untold stories of luminous kindness of ordinary people. Amidst both raging fires and settled hate, hundreds risked their own lives and those of their families and their homes to save innocent men and women, boys and girls, and even today many generously help the betrayed and shattered people heal and rebuild.

In Koha, a village not far from Ahmedabad, more than 110 mortally afraid Muslim men, women and children cowered for many hours amidst standing crops. In the wake of the rumours that people of their faith had burnt a train compartment of Hindu pilgrims in neighbouring Godhra, armed mobs including their neighbours had looted and torched their homes.

As darkness fell, they made their way to the thatch and earth home of Dhuraji and Babuben Thakur at the edge of their small seven-acre farmland and begged for shelter for just one night. Neither Dhuraji nor Babuben hesitated even for a moment and opened their doors and hearts to all 110 of their traumatized, wearied, now homeless neighbours. The next morning they offered to leave for the relief camp, but their hosts would not hear of it. 'This is your home,' they assured them. 'As long as God has given to us, we will share whatever we have with you.' They opened their entire stores of rice and bajra for the whole year, and ensured that all were fed for a full ten days that they lived in the sanctuary of their home. The women of the family brought out all their clothes, and would form a human wall around their well as the Muslim women bathed each day.

Dhuraji gathered his extended family from the village and kept constant watch for their guests, for ten nights and days, armed only with their peasant sickles. The women and children were persuaded to sleep inside the house, while the Thakur women slept in the open fields and the men kept vigil through the long, cold nights. They were unshaken by threats from their Hindu neighbours, who sent them bangles to taunt them, set fire to their haystacks, and one night even stole in through the darkness to set their house on fire, a conflagration they all doused just in time.

Still, Dhuraji and his wife Babuben were perfect hosts, just as though these were normal times. They tried to meet every need of their guests, to make them feel constantly welcome. Dhuraji's sons would set out in their tractors and bring back large stocks of bidis for the men, tea for the women and milk for the children. Years later, those whose lives they saved remembered fondly that seeing them in gloom, Dhuraji even hired a VCR and showed them Hindi films to buoy their spirits.

At the end of ten days, it was they who insisted that they

must shift to the relief camp. Dhuraji and Babuben tried to persuade them to stay as long as they could not return to rebuild their own homes, but they were adamant. Dhuraji finally organized tractors and a police escort and saw them safely to the camp. He visited them regularly at the camp as well, and the women recall that his eyes would often fill with tears when he saw their children lose weight in the austere rigours of the camp and stand in lines for watery tea.

Four years later, when I met Dhuraji and Babuben, they were embarrassed that I thought what they had done was magnificent. When I pressed them about why they did what they did, Dhuraji thought a long time before he replied, 'How could I bear it that people of my village are treated this way?' He added firmly, 'This village belongs to the Muslims as much as it belongs to me.'

I asked if they regretted that they lost their entire year's stock of grain in ten days. Dhuraji replied, 'God ensured that we get a good harvest after our guests left, and since that day, our grain stocks have never fallen empty.' Babuben added, 'Their good wishes and prayers have strengthened us. Don't you see greenery everywhere?'

I did.

A few hundred kilometres away, in the remote village of Nanaposhina in Sabarkantha district, white-haired Walibhai, a stubborn, ageing agricultural worker, was helplessly enraged when his house was looted and burnt by his young neighbours, boys who had grown up before his eyes. He fiercely insisted on remaining in the village to guard the shell of scorched walls which was all that was left of his home, although he forced his sons who drive taxies and his wife Mariam to the safety of a relief camp.

He sat awake weeping the whole night in the shadow of his collapsed home. The next morning, it hit him afresh that he had lost everything overnight. He did not even have a lota or water pitcher to take to the fields. A Thakur boy who walked past felt sorry for the old man and quietly gave him his lota and left without a word. Walibhai recalls that it was with this small act of kindness that that he was able to begin his life again. His neighbour, a Patel, called him shortly after to say that there was a phone call for him. His daughter-in-law informed him that she had had a son the night before. 'We have lost everything,' he cried to her. She contradicted him firmly, 'You are saved. This means we have everything.'

He found a broken piece of an earthen pot on which to make himself some rotis, refusing to hide any more, glowering at people as they threatened him. But the wife of his Patel neighbour insisted that she would feed him, and for eight days she defied the angry opposition of many in her village to openly bring him food and tea as he guarded his home. 'What has happened is wrong,' she said simply to everyone who protested.

Four years later, when we visited him, the walls of his home still were burnt, but there were shining corrugated sheets screwed on to the roof. 'See my good fortune', he said to me. 'Rambhai Adivasi was not even a close friend. We only used to sit and talk together sometimes. But when he saw my burnt house some months later, he cried. Without a word, he went home, bought these sheets for six thousand rupees, hired workers and a tractor to transport these here. The workers told me they had instructions to not heed my objections, and to fix the iron sheets. That is how I have a roof over my head today! Look at my good fortune, my friend.'

Despite this, Walibhai continued to feel utterly betrayed that his own neighbours had attacked, looted and torched his home. He had tried to file a police complaint with the names of all the attackers, but the policeman threatened him with his life if he persisted with his complaint. Fearing for the safety of his family, Walibhai had succumbed then to the police threats. The police complaint claimed, identical to complaints lodged all across Gujarat in 2002, that the enraged mob that attacked his home was anonymous. The case was closed, because it is impossible to catch faceless attackers. Four years later, Walibhai was among the first to grasp the opportunity offered by community justice workers of Nyayagrah to name fourteen tormentors in his now reopened case. The elders of the village gathered at his home to offer him money, and persuade him to not persist with his police statement. Even the Muslim residents were angry that his foolhardy stubbornness threatened their ever-precarious safety.

The elders said to Walibhai, 'The boys you are naming to the police grew up before your eyes. Why don't you forgive them? They are like your sons.' Walibhai replied, 'Yes, they are like my sons. I want to forgive them. I only wish for them to call a village meeting, and to publicly seek my forgiveness. I pledge that I will not pursue my complaint with the police after that.' They replied that they were willing to give him any amount of money, but they were not willing to publicly ask for forgiveness. Walibhai replied that in that case, he would not touch their money, and whatever were the consequences, he would pursue the criminal case to the end. He made his statement before the police, and as a consequence, the fourteen youth tormentors were arrested.

I met Walibhai and his wife Mariam after the arrests, which had created a minor earthquake in social relations in the entire region. After his statement to the police, he was boycotted completely by both the Hindu and Muslim residents of his village. Completely isolated in his remote village, but fiercely proud and elated, he declared, 'I don't care if they hack me to pieces now. I feel I am at last restored as a human being.'

I realized then that the path to reconciliation and forgiveness is an arduous and tortuous one. It is a path on which people who live with hate and fear, those who perpetrated and survived violence, must meet. They must exchange truth, however

fearful and ugly, and remorse and forgiveness. Together, they
must help rebuild shattered lives and trust, establish equality
before the law, and then find ways to heal and to live together
and eventually, one day, maybe even to love again.

Annexure:
The Verdicts of Citizens' Reports

DETAILS OF SAVAGERY

The majority of citizens groups' reports elaborate exhaustively the harrowing details of the savagery. The report of the CCT comprising retired senior judges of the Supreme Court, senior advocates and activists, marshalled evidence which shows 'how in the macabre dance of death, human beings were quartered and the killing protracted while the terrorised survivors looked on; the persons targeted were dragged or paraded naked through the neighbourhood; victims were urinated upon, before being finally cut to pieces and burnt.[1] Hundreds of testimonies before us show how this manner and method of killing has left an indelible imprint on the minds of the survivors.' It notes that, 'the burning alive of victims was widespread. A particularly tragic incident was one in which when six-year-old Irfan asked for water, his assailants at Naroda Patiya made him forcibly drink kerosene, or some other inflammable liquid, before a lit match was thrown inside his gullet to make him explode within.' (CCT 2002: 6)

The report of the People's Union for Democratic Rights (PUDR), Delhi, collected evidence of brutalities from the worst-affected districts in the north-east–south-west axis of rural Gujarat.[2] Discerning a recurring pattern in the narratives, it focuses on the 'chilling monotony in each account of killing, burning, arson, raping, maiming, looting. A drab sameness in the cries of "*Maaro, kaapo, baalo*" (Kill! Hack! Burn!) shouted by Hindu mobs, in the accounts of police inaction, in the peculiar mixture of bewilderment, anger, fear and hopelessness in the eyes of victims in relief camps across the districts we visited. Accounts of incidents occurring in places far apart bear a frightening resemblance to each other in the brutality of the massacres of Muslim men, women and children and the participation of their own Hindu neighbours in these attacks.'

In a sample of incidents detailed by PUDR, in Pandarwada village of Panchmahals, the killings were organized in amazing detail. 'A mammoth 15,000 strong mob of Bhils from nearly villages was mobilized and went on a rampage for nearly a whole day, looting Muslim goods and killing livestock and people. Local leaders then deliberately deceived the Muslims by offering shelters in their homes and fields, and then leading mob attacks to hack or burn them, killing thirty-eight. All the survivors of the attack, including women and small children, fled from the village and hid wherever they could, in the hills and jungle, some for three to four long days, without food or water, young children chewing the leaves of the trees to survive. Each had to run and hide from violent mobs waiting for them on all roads, and run a little more, and hide again, to save his or her life.'

In Radhikpur village in Dahod, again adivasis set fire to Muslim homes. Local villagers blocked all paths, and left twenty dead. As some ran into the forest, 'Shamim who had delivered a day before and her child were also killed. Bilkis, a five-month pregnant young woman was gang raped by three men from her village. Her three-year-old daughter was snatched away from her and killed in front of her.' In a particularly

gruesome incident reported from Sardarpura village in district
Mehsana, 'Thirty-one people, mostly women and children had
taken shelter in a house in the Sheikh locality. The mob
surrounded the house, locked them into a room, and threw
acid at them through openings in the room. The metal
conductor, an iron rod attached by a wire to the newly installed
halogen light, was shoved inside the room packed with Muslims
and electric current passed through it. The device was moved
around in the room and used to electrocute twenty-nine
persons to death. Two children who fell beneath the pile of
bodies of the dead survived the attack.'

Like several other reports, the CCT documents extensively
the specific targeting of women and young girls, as well as
children. Evidence before the tribunal shows that women have
'suffered the most bestial forms of sexual violence, including
rape, gang rape, insertion of objects into their bodies, stripping,
and molestation. A majority of the women who suffered this
violence were then burnt alive. Amongst the survivors, many
have spoken about the assaults but many have been silenced,
for fear of further attacks and for fear of censure from their
own families and community. Besides the lack of faith in the
system of justice, the humiliation faced by women who dare
challenge taboos and demand punishment for gender crimes
like rape have silenced the natural cry for retribution and
justice.'

The tribunal observes that, 'a distinct, tragic and ghastly
feature of the state sponsored carnage unleashed against a
section of the population, the Muslim minority in Gujarat,
was the systematic sexual violence unleashed against young
girls and women. Rape was used as an instrument for the
subjugation and humiliation of a community. A chilling
technique, absent in pogroms unleashed hitherto but very
much in evidence this time in a large number of cases, was the
deliberate destruction of evidence. Barring a few, in most

instances of sexual violence, the women victims were stripped and paraded naked, then gangraped, and thereafter quartered and burnt beyond recognition. According to the evidence recorded by the Tribunal, the leaders of the mobs (many of whom have been identified) even raped young girls, some as young as eleven years old. The young girls were made to remove their clothes in front of 1000–2000 strong mobs who humiliated and terrorized the girls. Thereafter, they were raped by ten men. After raping them, the attackers inserted sharp swords, knives or hard objects into their bodies to torture them before burning them alive. In the many bouts of communally incited pogroms that have taken place in different parts of the country, never has there been this depth of perversion, sickness and inhumaneness. Even a twenty-day-old infant, or a foetus in the womb of its mother, was not spared.'

The unprecedented bestiality of mass sexual violence on women is recorded with particular sensitivity by various investigating women's groups. In one such report 'The Survivors Speak' there are several wrenching testimonies of mass rape.[3] Sultani, for instance, from village Eral in Panchmahals, speaks of how, escaping from a mob, '[I] fell behind as I was carrying my son, Faizan. The men caught me from behind and threw me on the ground. Faizan fell from my arms and started crying. My clothes were stripped off by the men and I was left stark naked. One by one the men raped me. All the while I could hear my son crying. I lost count after three. They then cut my foot with a sharp weapon and left me there in that state.' A mother, Medina, from the same village testifies that, 'two villagers pulled away' her own daughter. 'My mind was seething with fear and fury. I could do nothing to help my daughter from being assaulted sexually and tortured to death. My daughter was like a flower, still to experience life. Why did they have to do this to her? What kind of men are these? The monsters tore my beloved daughter to pieces.

After a while, the mob was saying cut them to pieces, leave no evidence. I saw fires being lit. After some time the mob started leaving. And it became quiet.'

Many reports refer to the horror of Kausar Bano. In the words of Siara Bano, reported in The Survivors Speak, 'What they did to my sister-in-law's sister Kausar Bano was horrific and heinous. She was nine months pregnant. They cut open her belly, took out her foetus with a sword and threw it into a blazing fire. Then they burnt her as well.' The Survivors Speak report describes this as a 'meta-narrative', a story told many times. 'Sometimes the details would vary—the foetus was dashed to the ground; the foetus was slaughtered with a sword; the foetus was swung on the point of the sword and then thrown into a fire. In all instances where extreme violence is experienced collectively, meta-narratives are constructed. Each victim is part of the narrative; their experience subsumed by the collective experience. Kausar is that collective experience— a meta-narrative of bestiality; a meta-narrative of helpless victimhood. There are a thousand Kausars. Members of the fact-finding team have seen photographic evidence of the burnt bodies of a mother and a foetus lying on the mother's belly, as if torn from the uterus and left on the gash. We do not know if that was Kausar Bano.'

Many reports describe the use of children as instruments of terror. The People's Union for Civil Liberties (PUCL), Vadodara, report on violence in the city, for instance, states: 'In what is surely the most perverse dimension of the violence, children were used to torture and terrorize victims. In one particular tragic incident in Tarsali, an old Muslim man was shown the head of his beheaded son on a tray before he was himself brutally slain. Another woman surrounded by a mob had to watch as her son, who had climbed up a tree to escape the mob, was brought down, his fingers cut off and the rest of his body dismembered in her presence, all before she herself was killed.'[4]

The impact of such merciless violence on children is excruciating even to imagine. Thirteen-year-old Azharuddin testifies, 'I saw Farzana being raped by Guddu Chara. Farzana was about thirteen years old. She was a resident of Hussain Nagar. They put a *saria* [rod] in Farzana's stomach. She was later burnt. Twelve-year-old Noorjahan was also raped. The rapists were Guddu, Suresh and Naresh Chara and Haria. I also saw Bhawani Singh, who works in the state Transport Department kill five men and a boy.'

An independent team of citizens, supported by Citizens' Initiative, attempted specifically to assess the impact of this trauma on children.[5] In 'The Next Generations' based on investigations with children in relief camps, they report: 'Some were tiny adults who seemed to have learnt the importance of narrating to the world the terrible horrors they had witnessed. They would talk to us stoically, then suddenly bury head in arm, when it came to the rape of a mother or an aunt. Others would break down howling when reminded of a beloved cat that had been brained by a hostile neighbour or a buffalo that had disappeared. Every minority camp also had at least one or two who sat with head drooping into neck after giving us his/her name and that of the only surviving parent or grandparent.

'Eight-year-old Saddam described to this team how men attacked and "then...then they stripped my mother naked...*usko nanga kar diya*". A nine-year old volunteered to explain to another women's team what *balatkar* [rape] means. "*Balatkaar ka matlab jab aurat ko nanga karte hain aur phir use jala deta hain* (Rape is when a woman is stripped naked and then burnt)" and then looked fixedly at the floor.' The Next Generation report goes on to observe: 'Only a child can tell it like it is. For this is what happened again and again in Naroda Patia—women were stripped, raped and burnt. Burning has now become an essential part of the meaning of rape.'

For some children, the sense of loss is more innocent, but no less profound. In 'The Survivors Speak', seven-year-old Shaheen 'can't understand why her loss is less important than others. Resentment is barely concealed in her innocent eyes. Because the looters who attacked her village, snatched away her most prized possessions—her toys. "*Ek cycle thi* (I had a cycle)," she says. But lest we don't appreciate the full extent of her loss, she quickly adds, "*Doosri cycle bhi thi* (I also had another cycle)." Now she is unstoppable. In barely audible tones, the list starts pouring out of her mouth—"*Ek kursi, ek vimaan. Ek choolah bhi tha. Chooleh pe roti banate the. Gudiya bhi thi*. (One chair, one aeroplane, one stove. I used to make *rotis* on my stove. I also had a doll)."' Are Hindus bad, we ask? "Yes," she nods, followed by a quick, "No." She thinks of Anita and Kamal, her friends in the village school in Atasumba. They are Hindus. She misses them.'

PLANNED POGROM

A second thread that runs through most reports is the systematic and planned character of the massacre, reflecting an elaborate sinister blueprint allegedly drawn up well before the horrific torching of the railway compartment in Godhra. As put in the PUDR report, 'the official use of the word "riot", evoking images of group clashes, is not just wrong but a deliberate effort to obfuscate the issue. What happened was a systematic effort to terrorize Muslims and reduce them to the status of second-class citizens by taking away their lives, livelihood and shelter. It was a genocide that was almost unprecedented in its spread and intensity, the degree of organization and attention to detail, and the extent to which representatives of the state participated in the attacks.'

The CCT notes on the basis of 'the extensive evidence recorded by the Tribunal, it is clear that Muslims from all social strata, rich and poor, were the prime targets for the state-sponsored pogrom unleashed all over the state of Gujarat. From cities and towns to villages, be it the question of life, dignity or property, barring few exceptions, Muslims were the sole target. While the targeting of economically better off Muslims was limited to their property, and damage was vast and extensive (the carnage in Gulbarg society, where former MP Ahsan Jafri was specifically targeted, being an exception), the lower middle class and the working class sector, be it in urban centres or villages, faced attacks on their life, property and dignity.'

Through the voluminous evidence presented before the tribunal, it estimated that, 'across Gujarat, over 1100 Muslim-owned hotels, the homes of not less that 1,00,000 families, over 15,000 small and big business establishments, around 3000 larri galas (handcarts), and over 5000 vehicles (private cars, trucks, taxis, autorickshaws) were badly damaged or completely destroyed in the attacks. These figures indicate the attempt to economically cripple a community on a scale unprecedented in the post-independence history of communal violence in the country.'

The advanced planning for the carnage is corroborated in many reports by certain common features in the pattern of mass violence which occurred simultaneously in far-flung regions of the state. As observed by a fact finding team set up by Sahmat, 'firstly the rioting mobs were huge ones and with a substantial segment properly trained for such activities.[6] In fact, they more resembled a militia rather than spontaneously mobilized fanatics. The premeditated nature of the attacks is indicated by the almost exclusive selection of Muslim commercial establishments, residential areas and individual residences. After the experience of earlier riots, most of the Muslim establishments had non-Muslim, mainly Hindu names. Yet the attackers reportedly had lists, and specifically targeted Muslim properties. In instance after instance, we saw

Muslim shops, workshops, and flats burnt and looted while the neighbouring Hindu owned properties were untouched.'

In similar tenor, an independent fact finding mission, noted that 'certain crucial aspects of the carrying out of the pogrom required systematic planning well in advance of the Godhra incident.[7] The lists the rioters possessed and used must have been compiled over time. The targeting of Muslim homes, institutions, establishments and shrines was very precise and accurate. Even when there was only one Muslim shop or home in a congested Hindu-dominated area, it was attacked, ransacked and burnt. Businesses that had Hindu or non-Muslim names, were identified and targeted along with others in which Muslims were minority or sleeping partners.'

The Editors Guild Fact Finding Mission, which included Dileep Padgaonkar, editor-in-chief of the *Times of India*, and respected senior journalist B.G. Verghese, also refers to 'the holocaust and the meticulous targeting of Muslim homes, mohallas, shops and establishments, factories, hotels and eateries and other economic assets as well as dargahs, mosques, shrines and kabristans.[8] Neighbouring Hindu properties were spared. Obviously these targets must have been marked out as even Muslim establishments with names like Tulsi Restaurant or Tasty Bakery largely catering to a Hindu clientele, were looted and fired.'

Various reports describe a frightening congruence in modes of attack. The CCT concludes: 'the evidence recorded before the Tribunal shows that, while Godhra provided the pretext, there was prior mobilization of men and materials, and an organization in place that made possible the systematic and calculated preparations that preceded many of the massacres'. It goes on to state: 'the evidence before the Tribunal clearly points to scores of key actors leading large mobs, fully aware of what they had to do and achieving their task with precision. This suggests the existence of a private, trained militia running into thousands in Gujarat. A militia, moreover, established and made fighting fit through training camps, distribution of weaponry and hate propaganda glorifying violence. Weapons used in attacks, such as swords, were of the same brand, and must obviously have been distributed in advance across large tracts of the state.'

The Sahmat report states, 'the modus operandi was often the same. Vehicles including trucks were brought to cart away the loot. In the cases of factories and commercial establishments that had strong grills and metal shutters, gas cutters were used to gain access. LPG cylinders were used to blow up residential rooms and shops. Thousands must have been used. Such massive provision of LPG cylinders must have involved official collusion, if not sanction.'

The PUCL, Vadodara, in its report describes the same pattern: 'the presence of large roving mobs, armed with swords, and raising slogans like *Jai Sri Ram* and *Jai Hanuman*, attacking Muslim houses and shops. Reports from various Muslim localities over the first two days of violence spoke of stoning, threatening, stabbing, and the use of swords by mobs. Swords were a prominent weapon employed to intimidate Muslims. Throughout the night of 28 February, terrified Muslims hid in their homes, or in some cases were sheltered by non-Muslim neighbours. Shops were set on fire by drilling holes in walls, pouring in inflammable chemicals and then setting them on fire so that they first smouldered and then burst into flames.'

The CCT identifies three categories of assailants to execute the operations. 'The leadership of large mobs running into thousands was provided by easily identifiable elected representatives of the BJP (including cabinet ministers), and others from the VHP, the Bajrang Dal and the RSS. These leaders quite often carried computer printouts of the names and addresses of Muslims homes and shops. Field operations were co-ordinated by a central command using mobile phones.

The second rung comprised of [sic] the chief executioners who wielded all the weapons—guns, trishuls, swords—and handled arsenals and supplies—petrol, diesel, kerosene, chemicals and gas cylinders—for starting fires. They moved around in vehicles loaded with chemicals and weapons. This was the group primarily responsible for the brutal killings, sexual assaults and other abuses. Muslim survivors from many villages told the Tribunal that these aggressors carried identical backpacks filled with pouches of chemicals. The planning was so elaborate that a particular group of people had been assigned only the task of loading guns. The third group was mainly involved in looting property from the houses and shops. In some of the tribal areas, this group consisted of Adivasis.'

Another menacing motif that characterized the mass violence across the state was the extensive religious and cultural desecration. As stated in the Sahmat report, 'along with the butchering of human lives, there has been widespread destruction of masjids and dargahs. Rough estimates suggest twenty odd mosques being demolished in Ahmedabad alone. As has been mentioned earlier, the major attacks were organized on 1st March and the pattern seems to suggest targeting of mosques in all parts of city, during the Friday prayers. In most of the places, Hindu idols were placed on the site of the mosques after demolishing them, thus converting them into temples a la VHP style. In many cases, liquor was consumed within the mosques and madrassas, and holy books burnt within madrassas. The small Hindu temple within the Muslim locality of *Sundaramnagar* which remained unharmed while its neighbouring mosque and madrassa were burnt and destroyed, stood in sharp contrast to the vandalism of the VHP rioters.'

However, these attacks on the mosques should not be seen only in terms of being acts of provocation meant to incite the Muslim minority by hurting religious sentiments. They were also accompanied by attacks on historical monuments. As chronicled in the Sahmat report, 'the famous 500-year-old masjid in Isanpur, which was an ASI monument, was destroyed with the help of cranes and bulldozers. The famous Urdu Poet Wali Gujarati's dargah was also razed to the ground at Shahibag in Ahmedabad. While a Hanuman shrine was built over its debris initially, all that was removed overnight and the plot was metalled and merged with the adjoining road. No authority claimed any knowledge about the entire episode. It is worth noting here that the Ahmedabad Municipal Corporation, which is responsible for the maintenance of all these structures, and for the building of roads, is run by the Congress with a near two-thirds majority.'

The CCT find this to be a common pattern across Gujarat. 'Mosques, dargahs, small shrines and other Muslim religious and cultural places were systematically destroyed and desecrated in the first seventy-two-hour round of violence all over Gujarat. Copies of the Koran and other religious books were despoiled and damaged in many places all over the city of Ahmedabad, in Vadodara, Ankleshwar and Bharuch and in many smaller towns and villages all over the state. In all, over 270 mosques and dargahs have been thus destroyed. In many cases "Jai Shri Ram!" was scrolled all over the desecrated shrines. In many shrines, idols of "Hulladiya Hanuman" (translated, it means "Riot Hanuman") were installed. This shows the cynical abuse of caste Hindu religious symbols as instruments of domination and subjugation of Muslims.'

According to the PUDR report, 'very often mosques and dargahs were attacked first. In Vasad (Anand district), a mosque and a dargah were flattened with a bulldozer. In Sanjeli (Dahod), the mosque was broken, set on fire, and abusive anti-Muslim slogans were written all over the walls. Saffron flags and Hanuman images in mosques and dargahs are routine sights in urban and rural areas. In Boru (Panchmahals), a dargah which Hindus from distant places also visited has been desecrated. Symbolic desecration of mosques and qurans followed by their actual destruction and burning of Muslim houses in village after village shows the systematic attempt to stamp out the cultural identity of Muslims. Threats issued to many Muslims trying to go back to their villages hinge upon their stopping the use of cultural symbols, even caps and beards for men and salwar kameez for women.'

Poignantly, the PUDR report also notes: 'Another pattern that has emerged throughout the region is that the Muslims in a number of places trusted their attackers.' The systematic betrayal of trust is founded in long years of systematic hate propaganda, which disseminates the most vicious bigotry, documented in many reports. This is summarized, for instance, in the CCT report: 'Widespread hate propaganda was conducted through pamphlets distributed by Hindu communal organizations in different areas in large numbers. The content of these included calls for the social and economic boycott of Muslims, warnings about Muslims constituting a danger to the survival of Hindus, urging Hindus to awaken and to decimate and drive Muslims out from India.'

The CCT records 'sinister preparation and planning for the Gujarat carnage long before the Godhra tragedy, by the Sangh Parivar affiliates, their leaders confident of impunity from the long arm of the law since they enjoyed the patronage of the ruling party'. It has specific and detailed evidence on the method of mobilization and training adopted by the VHP and Bajrang Dal whereby huge mobs surfaced so promptly all over the state during the carnage. It also explains the ability of these organizations to collect youngsters, indoctrinated with misconceptions and with hatred in their hearts, who were available at a signal from their leaders to commit murder, loot, arson and rape, and defy all laws. It notes with horror and outrage, the level of impunity that such unlawful, armed organizations have come to enjoy in BJP-ruled Gujarat.

Further the tribunal states, 'The constant invocation of caste Hindu symbols, militant and aggressive posturing, the possession of trishuls and swords and regular weapons' training were elements of the methodical preparation of these cadres. At the advanced stage of training, the more seasoned members were told they would have to participate in fights or riots (ladhai-jhagda, danga-fasaad) whenever necessary. The tribunal collected concrete information about the kind of mental training and brainwashing imparted to young men at the secret, weekly meetings—'We were told that until now it is the Muslims who have been harassing Hindus. They have molested Hindu sisters and Hindu daughters. In Hindi films today, all the top heroes are Muslims, but there are no Muslim heroines. It is Muslims who are forging ahead in our country. They don't let their daughters out in public but they spoil our Hindu daughters. Muslims are the ones who always use force. Our country was once a Hindu nation. The Muslims invaded us by force, married our mothers and our daughters and converted us to Islam.'

PARTISAN ROLE OF THE STATE

Another blood-drenched chord that runs through the terrifying reconstruction of the mass violence in Godhra and its bloody aftermath in various citizens groups' report is the unashamed partisan role of the state authorities, the political leadership, the police and civil authorities. As summarized by noted historian K.N. Pannikar on 9 March, 2002 after his visit to Ahmedabad (quoted in the Sahmat report), 'What happened in Ahmedabad and other towns and villages in Gujarat is not a spontaneous action. The methods used for destruction of life and property presupposes a fairly well organized preparation. It is clear that many incidents during these last ten days could not have happened without such a preparation.

In a way it indicates a long-term process of communalisation and brutalisation of society. A major issue which society has to face is the influence of brutality, which appears to have conquered the minds of men. This is the result of the systematic and long-term atrocities of communal organizations and heightened by the irrational and emotional coercion of the people by both the VHP and the RSS.'

The openly partisan, and even deliberately provocative role of the state leadership is typically summarised by the independent fact-finding mission as follows: 'the government statements immediately after Godhra virtually accusing the Ghanchis of Singhal Faliya of acting as Pakistani ISI agents, and their decision to publicise the transporting of the charred bodies to Ahmedabad for public funeral, can only be seen as a cynical attempt to foment communal tension and hysteria essential for the attacks that inevitably followed. This was compounded by the state government's sanction and support for the VHP bandh and their signal to the bureaucracy and police to minimise their intervention. Since then the government has systematically tried to cover up, minimise, and even justify, the extent of violence, while protecting the guilty and those guilty of dereliction of duty. This is why the events of February–March 2002 can only be called a state-sponsored pogrom.'

There is extensive and deeply damaging documentation of the criminal partisanship of the state police. The PUDR report states that, 'police action has ranged from active collusion with the mobs to silent inaction in the face of cognizable and serious offences; from state apathy towards formulating and executing preventive measures to the unjustified and frequently biased resort to gunfire'. The CCT is even more categorical that there is overwhelming evidence that 'clearly establishes the absolute failure of large sections of the Gujarat police to fulfil their constitutional duty and prevent mass massacre, rape and arson—in short, to maintain law and order. Worse still is the evidence of their active connivance and brutality, their indulgence in vulgar and obscene conduct against women and children in full public view. It is as if, instead of being impartial keepers of the rule of law, they were a part of the Hindutva brigade targeting helpless Muslims.'

The tribunal also indicts the police for doing nothing since 1998 to stem the open dissemination of incendiary and provocative literature, inciting cadres of pseudo-Hindu militant organizations to rape, humiliate, destroy and kill. They turned a blind eye to the open, systematic collection of data on Muslim lives and properties. These organizations for four years prior to the carnage openly distributed trishuls and daggers and ran training camps, even for women and children, which the police refused to resist or halt. Likewise, the independent fact-finding mission notes: 'it is a measure of the virtual breakdown of large areas of police functioning that intelligence reports of this Hindutva planning were either not compiled or ignored by higher-ups. These types of preparations should not have gone unnoticed since, at the very least, hundreds must have been involved. Further, this mass movement of men, materials and vehicles could easily have been curbed by decisive police action, which would have led to a dramatic fall in casualties, rape and destruction of property. Virtually no preventive arrests were made, further emboldening the mobs. Later arrests reportedly had a disproportionate number of Muslims.'

Even the NHRC made several observations about the state government's failures.[9] 'The violence in the state, which was initially claimed to have been brought under control in seventy two hours, persisted in varying degree for over two months, the toll in death and destruction rising with the passage of time. Despite the measures reportedly taken by the state government, which are recounted in its report of 12 April 2002, that report itself testifies to the increasing numbers who died or were injured or deprived of their liberty and compelled to seek shelter in relief camps. That report [of the state government] also testifies to the assault on the dignity and worth of the human person, particularly of women and children, through acts of rape and other humiliating crimes of violence and cruelty... [and] that many were deprived of their livelihood and capacity to sustain themselves with dignity. The facts, thus, speak for themselves, even as recounted in the 12 April 2002 report of the state government itself.'

Once the violence broke out, innumerable testimonies in virtually every report point to appalling inaction or active incitements to violence by police authorities. Even the NHRC notes that the communal marauders were widely reported to have been 'singling out certain homes and properties for death and destruction in certain districts—sometimes within view of police stations and personnel...' The CCT notes that, 'the Panchmahal and Dahod police were party and privy to the burning alive and hacking of villagers. The police posted at Anjanwa, Mora, Pandharwada villages, as also those near Limkheda and Limwada and Fatehpura (Dahod district) did nothing to stop the killings. The Mehsana district police were also guilty of the same misconduct, when they failed to prevent massacres like the ones at Sardarpura, Visnagar and Unjha. Similarly, in Anand and Kheda districts where massacres have taken place, the police presence was of no help. Detailed testimonies recorded from Ankleshwar and Bharuch also reveal complete dereliction of duty by the police.'

The tribunal report goes on to reflect on the official admission by the Gujarat police 'that it killed more Muslims than Hindus in its ostensible attempts to stop what was clearly targeted Hindu violence against Muslims. Of the 184 people who died in police firing since the violence began, 104 are Muslims, says a report drafted by Gujarat police force itself. This statistic substantiates the allegations of riot victims from virtually every part of the state that not only did the local police not do anything to stop the Hindu mobs; they actually turned their guns on the helpless Muslim victims'. The Sahmat report quotes testimonies from many survivors of the Naroda Patia massare of 'how the SRP misguided a large group of people who were trying to escape into a trap, where the mob killed them and threw the bodies into a well. Most of the dead bodies were charred or mutilated beyond recognition and an overwhelming majority of the survivors did not manage to have access to the bodies of their relatives and perform the last rites in a dignified manner.'

The Sahmat Report goes on to note that, 'the Police Commissioner in Ahmedabad commanded a total of 10,000 men including 3000 armed men, along with 16 companies of SRP. Yet mobs of up to 5000 and more men were allowed to run amuck, loot, rape, beat, murder while the police stood by, when it did not actually abet the mobs. As one senior police officer told us, the problem was not lack of force, but lack of will.' The graffiti 'left behind by the rioters on the charred walls of the completely burnt madarasa at Sundaramnagar boasted of the police support: *Yeh andar ki bat hai Police hamarey saath hai* (This is inside information, the police is with us).'

The CCT points out grave acts of omission, which enabled the heinous crime at Godhra and its bloody aftermath of 'rage, revenge and violence' to unfold. It points out: 'Gujarat and indeed the whole country was on red alert due to the aggressive mobilisation by the VHP for building the temple at Ayodhya. In Mumbai, the police made as many as 8000 preventive arrests in the first week of March, to keep the situation under strict control. In contrast, even after Godhra happened, the Gujarat police arrested only two persons in Ahmedabad, both of whom were Muslims.'

Even in Godhra, it finds that, 'there was utter and complete failure of law and order maintenance and governance, particularly given the chequered communal history of the town. An investigation into the background of Godhra shows that when disturbances erupted in 1965, the then collector promptly arrested both Muslims and Hindus whose names appeared in FIRs and within a couple of days the disturbances were curbed. Even after the October 1980 disturbances, the then collector, Smt. S.K. Verma immediately put the miscreants behind bars. If a similar, no-nonsense and non-partisan approach had followed the Godhra incident of February 27, by promptly apprehending the suspected criminals, tension would have been contained. And the chances of a vengeful and highly organized spree of retaliatory killings that demonstrate every element of ethnic cleansing and genocide, would have been pre-empted. That this did not happen suggests a lack of intent on the part of those in government, to take prompt preventive measures in order to de-escalate the situation. In December 1992, a similar incident of provocation had occurred at Palej near Vadodara, but at that time, the state police cracked down on the Shiv Sainiks who had abused and provoked passengers and residents and thus squashed potential communal trouble within hours.'

The PUDR investigation found that, 'in a number of cases under the cover of controlling mobs, the police has shot Muslims who were being attacked, rather than their Hindu attackers'. It states that, 'there is no other explanation except that the police firings were communally motivated. Even in the instances where there was no overt communal bias there was a tendency to view the attacking mobs and the attacked people attempting to protect their lives and homes with the same yardstick, as criminals on an equal footing.'

An anguished police officer, V.N. Rai, respected for his integrity and courageous activism for a non-partisan police force, wrote an open letter titled 'A Call to Conscience' to his colleagues in the police force (quoted in Communalism Combat Report).[10]

> I am writing to you at a very difficult time as an Indian Police Service officer and with a sense of anguish. The recent events related to the communal holocaust in Gujarat are a matter of great concern for the country and should inspire serious introspection among all of us IPS officers. The terrible carnage that occurred at Godhra was an early warning of the fact that big events of communal destruction could occur the next day all over the state and the expectation from a professional police force was that it would oppose all actions of revenge and counter-violence with all the force that it could muster. But this did not happen. Not only was the police unsuccessful in containing the violence of the next few days but, it seemed, that in many places policemen were actively encouraging the rioters. The failure of the police should not be attributed to the lower ranks but must be seen as a failure of leadership, that is, a failure of the IPS.

The CCT recorded confidential evidence which corroborates that the state inaction and complexity in the mass violence after Godhra was systematically planned at the highest levels of the state. It states, 'senior ministers from Shri Modi's cabinet organized a meeting late in the evening on February 27, in Lunavada village of Sabarkantha district. Shri Ashok Bhatt, the state health minister and minister Prabhat Singh Chauhan from Lunavada attended. At this meeting, a diabolical plan was drawn and disseminated to the top fifty leaders of the BJP/RSS/BD/VHP, on the method and manner in which the seventy-two-hour-long carnage that followed was to be carried out.'

Even the NHRC makes reference to the 'local factors and players', in respect of whom the commission sought specific information, but the reply of the state government was silent. It refers to 'numerous eye-witness and media reports—including allegations specifically made to the Commission and communicated to the state government—which identify and name specific persons as being involved in the carnage, sometimes within the view of police stations and personnel. The reply (of the state government) makes no effort whatsoever to rebut the allegations made against such persons, or to indicate the action taken by the state government against those specifically named for participating in the egregious violation of human rights that occurred, or for inciting the acts of violence that resulted in murder, arson, rape and the destruction of lives and property'. It adds: 'The report of the state government of 12 April 2002 once again fails to make the necessary identification of these persons. It also fails to rebut the repeatedly made allegation that senior political personalities—who have been named—were seeking to influence the working of police stations by their presence within them.'

According to confidential evidence recorded by the CCT, 'these instructions were blatantly disseminated by the government, and in most cases, barring a few sterling exceptions, methodically carried out by the police and the IAS administration. There is no way that the debased levels of violence that were systematically carried out in Gujarat could have been allowed, had the police and district administration, the IPS and the IAS, stood by its constitutional obligation and followed Service Rules to prevent such crimes.'

Endnotes

Chapter 2: To Love Again: Paths to Reconciliation

[1] B. Rajeshwari, 'Communal Riots in India: A Chronology (1947-2003)'. New Delhi: Institute of Peace and Conflict Studies, 2004.

[2] Amartya Sen, *The Argumentative Indian: Writings on Indian History* (London: Allen Lane, 2005). Sen traces the importance of respect for diversity, in a coherent manner, from the time of Asoka's reign (3 BC) to the present.

[3] Charles Hauss, 'Reconciliation' in *Beyond Intractability*. Eds Guy Burgess and Heidi Burgess. Boulder: Conflict Research Consortium, 2003. http://www.beyondintractability.org/essay/reconciliation/.

[4] United Nations, *Religion an Reconciliation Backgrounder*, Http://www.tcd.ie/ise//postgraduate/reconcileBACKGROUNDER.pdf

[5] Author in conversation with Pratiksha Baxi, a law scholar.

[6] Brandon Hamber and Hugo van der Merve, 'Rainbow of Reconciliation' in *New People*, No. 55. 1998. Also, Hugo vander Merwe, Polly Dewhirst, and Brandon Hamber, 'Non Governmental Organizations and the Truth and Reconciliation Commission: An Impact Assessment'. South Africa: Centre for Study of Violence and Reconciliation, 1999.

[7] David Bloomfield, 'Reconciliation: An Introduction' in *Reconciliation after Violent Conflict: A Handbook*. Eds David Bloomfield, Teresa Barnes and Luc Huyse. Stockholm:

International Institute for Democracy and Electoral Assistance, 2003.

[8] Stef Vandeginste, 'Reparation' in *Reconciliation after Violent Conflict: A Handbook*. Eds David Bloomfield, Teresa Barnes and Luc Huyse. Stockholm: International Institute for Democracy and Electoral Assistance, 2003.

[9] J.S. Bandukwala, 'Glimmer in dark Gujarat?' 14 November 2007, http://www.indianexpress.com/news/glimmer-in-dark-gujarat/238738/.

Chapter 3: Imposed Forgiveness?: Learning from South Africa

[1] UnitedNations,*ReligionanReconciliationBackgrounder*,Http://www.tcd.ie/ise//postgraduate/reconcileBACKGROUNDER.pdf

[2] Priscilla B. Hayner, *Unspeakable Truths: Confronting State Terror and Atrocity*. New York: Routledge, 2001.

[3] Luc Huyse, 'The Process of Reconciliation' in *Reconciliation after Violent Conflict: A Handbook*. Eds David Bloomfield, Teresa Barnes and Luc Huyse. Stockholm: International Institute for Democracy and Electoral Assistance, 2003.

[4] Desmond M. Tutu, *No Future Without Forgiveness*. New York: Doubleday, 1999.

[5] David A. Crocker, 'Retribution and Reconciliation'. http://www.publicpolicy.umd.edu/IPPP/Winter-Spring00/retribution_and_reconciliation.htm. Institute for Philosophy and Public Policy, 2000.

[6] Sumanta Banerjee, 'Reconciliation Without Justice'. http://www.epw.org.in. 17 May 2003.

[7] Laure-Hélène Piron and Zaza Curran, 'Public Policy Responses to Exclusion: Evidence from Brazil, South Africa and India'. London: Overseas Development Institute, 2005.

[8] Luc Huyse, 'The Process of Reconciliation' in *Reconciliation after Violent Conflict: A Handbook*. Eds David Bloomfield, Teresa Barnes and Luc Huyse. Stockholm: International Institute for Democracy and Electoral Assistance, 2003.

[9] ibid.

[10] ibid.

[11] A comprehensive account of communal riots in India including the findings of these commissions can be found in Asghar Ali Engineer, *Communal Riots After Independence—A Comprehensive Account*. New Delhi: Shipra Publications, 2003.

[12] Paul Brass, *The Production of Hindu–Muslim Violence in Contemporary India*. New Delhi: Oxford University Press, 2003. Also, Asghar Ali Engineer, Ed., *Communal Riots in Post-Independence India*. Hyderabad: Sangam Books, 1991, and Ashutosh Varshney, *Ethnic Conflict and Civic Life in India: Hindus and Muslims in India*. Yale: Yale University Press, 2003.

Chapter 4: In Defiant Denial: Blockading Truth

[1] Ashish Khetan, 'Voyager between Two Worlds', *Tehelka*, 3 November 2007.

Chapter 5: Frozen Compassion: Celebrating the Massacre

[1] Tridip Suhrud, 'Gujarat's Home Made Hitler: Man, Mask And Modi', *Tehelka*, 19 January 2008.

[2] D.P. Bhattacharya, 'Modi Chalisa, A Disturbing Trend', www.expressindia.com, 9 January 2008.

Chapter 6: States of Trauma: Failures of Reparation

[1] Stef Vandeginste, 'Reparation' in *Reconciliation after Violent Conflict: A Handbook*. Eds David Bloomfield, Teresa Barnes and Luc Huyse. Stockholm: International Institute for Democracy and Electoral Assistance, 2003.

[2] ibid.

[3] Concerned Citizens Tribunal, 'An Inquiry into the Carnage in Gujarat, Vol. II: Crime against Humanity, Findings and Recommendations'. Ahmedabad: Concerned Citizens Tribunal, 2002.

[4] This report is not available in the public domain yet. I have applied under the Right to Information Act for a full set of documents, which will be made available in the public domain.

[5] Report to the Commissioners of the Supreme Court in the case CWP/196/2002 dated 21 November 2006 (mimeo).

[6] Centre for Social Justice, 'A Report of the Internally-Displaced in Gujarat Due to Communal Violence', Ahemdabad: Centre for Social Justice, 2004.

[7] Rejoinder to the reply filed by the state of Gujarat by way of affidavit dated 4 January 2006 (para 11) in reply to the interim application filed by Harsh Mander in CRL. MP. no. 9236/2005, CRL. MP. no. 3741 & 3742/2004 and Writ petition (CRL.) no. 109/2003 in the matter of National Human Rights Commission versus the state of Gujarat and others.

[8] Letter to Harsh Mander, Special Commissioner of the Supreme Court from Dr S.K. Nanda, Principal Secretary, Government of Gujarat, dated 21 November 2002 (mimeo).

[9] The survey was financially supported by Oxfam India, and conducted by the community justice workers (nyaya pathiks), who work with a people's campaign for legal justice and reconciliation, Nyaygrah, implemented by Aman Biradari, Lawyers' Collective and Yusuf Meheralli Centre.

[10] Centre for Social Justice, 'A Report of the Internally-Displaced in Gujarat Due to Communal Violence', Ahemdabad: Centre for Social Justice, 2004.

[11] like Jan Vikas and Action Aid India.

[12] mimeo

Chapter 7: In Wistful Longing: Vignettes of a Counterfeit Peace

[1] Talati is a local government official.

Chapter 8: Failures of Justice: Subversion of Law Enforcement

[1] In the Zahira Habibiullah Sheikh versus state of Gujarat case, better known as the Best Bakery case.

Chapter 9: Diary Jottings: Living with Injustice in 'Peaceful' Gujarat

[1] Press Trust of India, 'Muslims are Not Repentant for Godhra: Vajpayee', www.rediff.com, 17 December 2002.

Chapter 10: Fighting Back: Legal Resistance to Injustice

[1] Interim application filed by Harsh Mander in CRL. MP. no. 9236/2005, CRL. MP. no. 3741 & 3742/2004 and Writ petition (CRL.) no. 109/2003 in the matter of National Human Rights Commission versus the state of Gujarat and others

[2] Amartya Sen, *The Argumentative Indian: Writings on Indian History* (London: Allen Lane, 2005) and Ashish Nandy (1990)

[3] *Gujarat: The Making of a Tragedy*, Ed. Siddharth Varadarajan. New Delhi: Penguin, 2002.

[4] Paul R. Brass, 'Organized Riots and Structured Violence in India', *The Hindu*, 23 August 2006.

[5] ibid.

[6] In the high court of Delhi. Civil Writ Petition No. 1429 of 1996. Decided on 05.07.1996. Appellants: Bhajan Kaur vs Respondent: Delhi Administration through the Lt. Governor Ravi Kumar Arora vs Union of India and Anr., 111 (2004) DLT 126; Javed Abidi vs Union of India and Ors., AIR 1999 SC 512; Kamla Devi (Smt.) vs Government of NCT of Delhi and Anr., 2004 IV AD (Delhi) 557; D.K. Basu vs state of West Bengal, (1997) 1 SCC 416; Nilabati Behera vs state of Orissa, (1993) 2 SCC 746; Rudul Sah vs state of Bihar; M.S. Grewal vs Deep Chand Sood,(2001) 8 SCC 151; state of Gujarat vs Hon'ble High Court of Gujarat, (1998) 7 SCC 392; Charan Lal Sahu vs Union of India, (1990) 1 SCC 613; M.V. Elisabeth vs Harwan Investment and Trading (P) Ltd., 1993 Supp (2) SCC 433; S.S. Ahluwalia vs Union of India and Ors., 2001 (2) Scale 495; Smt. Shyama Devi vs Government of NCT of Delhi and Ors., 78 (1999) DLT 827; Uphar Tragedy and Ors. vs Union of India and Ors., 2003 (68) DRJ 128; Punjab Istri Sabha and Ors. vs Surjit Singh Barnala, Chief Minister, Punjab and Anr., 1990 ACJ 1064; Lata Wadhwa

and Ors. vs state of Bihar and Ors., JT 2001 (6) SC 431; Ward vs James, (1965) 1 All ER 563; R.D. Hattangadi vs Pest Control (India) (P) Ltd., (1995) 1 SCC 551; Nagappa vs Gurudayal Singh and Ors., (2003) 2 SCC 274; K.S.R.T.C. vs Mahadeva Shetty and Anr., AIR 2003 SC 4172

Chapter 11: From Satyagrah to Nyayagrah: Justice for Reconciliation and Healing

[1] From *The Sayings of Muhammad* (Saheeh Muslim Hadees)
[2] Ashis Nandy, 'Birth Pangs', *Times of India*, 14 August 2006.
[3] This testimony was made to filmmaker Akanksha Joshi, who took photographs to profile courage and compassion in Gujarat.
[4] Also made to Akanksha Joshi.

Annexure: The Verdicts of Citizens' Reports

[1] Concerned Citizens Tribunal. 'An Inquiry into the Carnage in Gujarat, Vol. II: Crime against Humanity, Findings and Recommendations'. Ahmedabad: Concerned Citizens Tribunal, 2002.

   The tribunal consisted of Justice V.R. Krishna Iyer, Justice P.B. Sawant, Justice Hosbet Suresh, Adv. K.G. Kannabiran, Aruna Roy, K.S. Subramanian, Prof. Ghanshyam Shah and Prof. Tanika Sarkar.

[2] People's Union for Democratic Rights. 'Maaro! Kaapo! Baalo!: State and Communalism in Gujarat'. Delhi: People's Union for Democratic Rights, 2002.

[3] Syeda Hameed, et al, 'How Has the Gujarat Massacre Affected Minority Women?: The Survivors Speak'. Ahmedabad: Citizen's Initiative, 2002.

   The panel consisted of Syeda Hameed, Ruth Manorama, Malini Ghose, Sheba George, Farah Naqvi and Mari Thekaekara.

[4] People's Union for Civil Liberties and Vadodara Shanti Abhiyan, 'Violence in Vadodara: A Report'. Vadodara: People's Union for Civil Liberties and Vadodara Shanti Abhiyan, 2002.

The members of fact-finding team were Chinu Srinivasan, Deeptha Achar, Iftikhar Ahmed, Johannes Manjrekar, Maya Valecha, Nandini Manjrekar, Raj Kumar Hans, Renu Khanna, Rohit Prajapati and Trupti Shah.

5   Kavita Panjabi, Krishna Bandopadhyay, and Bolan Gangopadhyay. 'The Next Generation: In the Wake of the Genocide—A Report on the Impact of the Gujarat Pogrom on Children and the Young'. Ahmedabad: Citizen's Initiative, 2002.

6   Kamal Mitra Chenoy, et al, 'Ethnic Cleansing in Ahmedabad: A Preliminary Report'. Ahmedabad: Sahmat, 10–11 March 2002.

The team members were Dr Kamal Mitra Chenoy, Vishnu Nagar, Prasenjit Bose and Vijoo Krishnan.

7   Kamal Mitra Chenoy, et al, 'Gujarat Carnage 2002: A Report to the Nation'. Ahmedabad: Centre for the Study of Culture and Society, 2002.

The team members were Dr Kamal Mitra Chenoy, S.P. Shukla, K.S. Subramanian and Achin Vanaik.

8   Aakar Patel, Dileep Padgaonkar, and B.G. Verghese. 'Fact Finding Mission'. New Delhi: Editor's Guild, 2002.

9   National Human Rights Commission, New Delhi. Suo Motu Case No.1150/6/2001-2002. 31 May 2002.

10 'Genocide Gujarat 2002', Communalism Combat, No. 77-78. Mumbai: March–April 2002.

References

Akbar, M. J. *Riot after Riot*. New Delhi: Penguin, 1991.

Banerjee, Sumanta. 'Reconciliation Without Justice'. http://www.epw.org.in. 17 May 2003.

Ben, Tal D. and G. Bennick. 'The Nature of Reconciliation as an Outcome and as a Process' in *From Conflict Resolution to Reconciliation*. Ed. Yaacov Bar-Simon-Tov. Oxford: Oxford University Press, 2003.

Bloomfield, David. 'On Good Terms: Clarifying Reconciliation' in Berghof Report No. 14. Berlin: Berghof Research Center for Constructive Conflict Management, 2006.

———— 'The Context of Reconciliation' in *Reconciliation after Violent Conflict: A Handbook*. Eds David Bloomfield, Teresa Barnes and Luc Huyse. Stockholm: International Institute for Democracy and Electoral Assistance, 2003.

———— 'Reconciliation: An Introduction' in *Reconciliation after Violent Conflict: A Handbook*. Eds David Bloomfield, Teresa Barnes and Luc Huyse. Stockholm: International Institute for Democracy and Electoral Assistance, 2003.

Brass, Paul. *The Production of Hindu–Muslim Violence in Contemporary India*. New Delhi: Oxford University Press, 2003.

Chandra, Bipan. *Communalism in Modern India*. India: Vikas Publishing House, 1984.

Chenoy, Kamal Mitra, et al. 'Ethnic Cleansing in Ahmedabad: A Preliminary Report'. Ahmedabad: Sahmat, 10–11 March 2002.

Chenoy, Kamal Mitra, et al. 'Gujarat Carnage 2002: A Report to the Nation'. Ahmedabad: Centre for the Study of Culture and Society, 2002.

Communal Riots in Post-Independence India. Ed. Asghar Ali Engineer. Hyderabad: Sangam Books, 1991.

Concerned Citizens Tribunal. 'An Inquiry into the Carnage in Gujarat, Vol. II: Crime against Humanity, Findings and Recommendations'. Ahmedabad: Concerned Citizens Tribunal, 2002.

Crocker, David A. 'Retribution and Reconciliation'. http://www.publicpolicy.umd.edu/IPPP/Winter-Spring00/retribution_and_reconciliation.htm. Institute for Philosophy and Public Policy, 2000.

D'Souza, Andreas. 'Reconciliation in Practice: The Indian Experience'. *Journal of the Henry Martyn Institute*, Vol. 21. Hyderabad: Henry Martin Institute, 2002.

Estrada-Hollenbeck, Mica. 'The Attainment of Justice through Restoration, Not Litigation: The Subjective Road to Reconciliation' in *Reconciliation, Coexistence and Justice in Interethnic Conflict: Theory and Practice*. Ed. Mohammed Abu-Nimer. Maryland: Lexington Books, 2001.

'Framework for Religious and Political Reconciliation'. http://www.bet-el.co.za/artikels/Framework%20For%20Reconciliation.pdf

Gobodo-Madikizela, Pumla. 'Beyond Truth and Reconciliation: Forgiveness' in *Peacework Magazine*. Massachusetts: American Friends Service Committee, May 1999. http://www.peaceworkmagazine.org/pwork/0599/0515.htm.

Hamber, Brandon, and Grainne Kelly. 'Reconciliation: A Working Definition'. Belfast: Democratic Dialogue, 2004.

Hamber, Brandon, and Hugo van der Merwe. 'Rainbow of Reconciliation' in *New People*, No. 55. 1998.

Hamber, Brandon. 'Healing' in *Reconciliation after Violent Conflict: A Handbook*. Eds David Bloomfield, Teresa Barnes and Luc Huyse. Stockholm: International Institute for Democracy and Electoral Assistance, 2003.

———— 'Truth: The Road to Reconciliation?' in *Cantilevers: Building Bridges for Peace*, Vol. 3. Johannesburg: Centre for Study of Violence and Reconciliation, 1997

Hameed, Syeda, et al. 'How Has the Gujarat Massacre Affected Minority Women?: The Survivors Speak'. Ahmedabad: Citizen's Initiative, 2002.

Hartwell, Marica Byrom. 'The Role of Forgiveness in Reconstructing Society after Conflict'. London: London School of Economics, 1998.

Hauss, Charles. 'Reconciliation' in *Beyond Intractability*. Eds Guy Burgess and Heidi Burgess. Boulder: Conflict Research Consortium, 2003. http://www.beyondintractability.org/essay/reconciliation/.

Huyse, Luc. 'The Process of Reconciliation' in *Reconciliation after Violent Conflict: A Handbook*. Eds David Bloomfield, Teresa Barnes and Luc Huyse. Stockholm: International Institute for Democracy and Electoral Assistance, 2003.

Kaufman, Edward. 'A Vehicle for Peace Building' in *People Building Peace II*. The Hague: European Centre for Conflict Prevention, 2005. www.peoplebuildingpeace.org/thestories/article.php?id=126&typ=theme&pid=30.

Lederach, John Paul. 'The Meeting Place' in *The Journey Toward Reconciliation*. Pennsylvania: Herald Press, 1999.

Mani, Rama. 'Balancing Peace with Justice in the Aftermath of Violent Conflict' in *Development*, Vol. 48, No. 3. Hampshire: Palgrave Macmillan, 2005.

National Human Right Commission. 'Orders and Proceedings of the Commission'. New Delhi: National Human Rights Commission, 2002.

Panjabi, Kavita, Krishna Bandopadhyay, and Bolan Gangopadhyay. 'The Next Generation: In the Wake of the Genocide—A Report on the Impact of the Gujarat Pogrom on Children and the Young'. Ahmedabad: Citizen's Initiative, 2002.

Patel, Aakar, Dileep Padgaonkar, and B.G. Verghese. 'Fact Finding Mission'. New Delhi: Editor's Guild, 2002.

People's Union for Civil Liberties and Vadodara Shanti Abhiyan. 'Violence in Vadodara: A Report'. Vadodara: People's Union for Civil Liberties and Vadodara Shanti Abhiyan, 2002.

People's Union for Democratic Rights. 'Maaro! Kaapo! Baalo!: State and Communalism in Gujarat'. Delhi: People's Union for Democratic Rights, 2002.

————'Gujarat Genocide: "Act Two" Six Months Later'. Delhi: People's Union for Democratic Rights, 2002.

Rai Vibhuti Narain. 'A Call to Conscience' in *Communalism Combat.* March–April 2002.

Rajeshwari, B. 'Communal Riots in India: A Chronology (1947-2003)'. New Delhi: Institute of Peace and Conflict Studies, 2004.

Taylor, Nick. 'Peace on the Line'. Manchester: *The Guardian*, 12 May 2004.

van der Merwe, Hugo, Polly Dewhirst, and Brandon Hamber. 'Non Governmental Organizations and the Truth and Reconciliation Commission: An Impact Assessment'. South Africa: Centre for Study of Violence and Reconciliation, 1999.

Vandeginste, Stef. 'Reparation' in *Reconciliation after Violent Conflict: A Handbook.* Eds David Bloomfield, Teresa Barnes and Luc Huyse. Stockholm: International Institute for Democracy and Electoral Assistance, 2003.

Varshney, Ashutosh. *Ethnic Conflict and Civic Life in India: Hindus and Muslims in India.* Yale: Yale University Press, 2003.

Acknowledgements

Ever since the carnage in Gujarat in 2002, I have written continually on the slaughter, its aftermath and consequences. My jottings have been published as numerous newspaper articles, including in the Hindustan Times and the Times of India, as well as in the Economic and Political Weekly, Frontline and Outlook. Portions of this book have appeared also in my books 'Cry My Beloved Country' published by Rainbow Publishers, and 'Towards Healing?' published by WISCOMP, and in various anthologies about Gujarat.

I am indebted to Manzoor Ghori and the Indian Muslim Relief and Charities, who raised individual donations to enable the work of Nyayagrah to progress these many years, along with friends like Nusrat Deen, Hyder Khan, Hameed, Imtiaz ud din, Saeed Patel, and Javed Sikander, and in India Anu Aga, Gulam Vahanvati, Titoo Ahluwalia and Azam Khan. I am grateful to Dr Meenakshi Gopinath and Sumona Dasgupta of WISCOMP and the Dalai Lama Foundation for their support for the research into reconciliation and justice in Gujarat. Indira Jaisingh and Anand Grover of Lawyers' Collective fought the entire legal battle for reopening 2000 closed cases in the Supreme Court for me pro bono. Girish Patel, G.G. Parekh, Rajni Bakshi, Ram Punyani, Syeda Hameed, NC Saxena, Mallika Sarabhai, Vijay Pratap, Ritu

Priya, Anand Grover, Bhushan Oza, Anand Yagnik, Sara Ahmed, Navsharan Kaur, Biraj Patnaik, Nina Ellinger and Viggo Brun are among those who extended assistance and affirmation to this work.

Ram Narayan Kumar, Angana Chatterji, Vrinda Grover and Manoj Jha undertook an invaluable external review of Nyayagrah, and helped sharpen our legal, political and ethical perspectives.

I thank my research supporters including Kiran Nanavati, Johanna Lokhande, Archana Rai, Nimisha Agarwal, M. Kumaran, Rafi P., Vijay Naugain, Swati Narayan and Tanveer Afaque, who contributed in many ways to this work. I also benefited greatly from invaluable detailed comments on various drafts of this manuscript received from many friends, including Pratiksha Baxi, Yasmeen Arif, Vinay Lal and Nina Ellinger.

I am grateful to my editors in Penguin, Ravi Singh and Shatarupa Ghoshal for their faith, support, warmth and patience

My wife Dimple and my daughter Suroor stood by me resolutely through these personally difficult and sometimes turbulent times. My parents and brother Raj also supported me with steady love and faith, through all of this.

I salute all those who bravely fought the politics of difference and divide and state impunity, including Shabnam Hashmi, Teesta Setalvad, Mukul Sinha and Gagan Sethi, and the workers of Citizens Initiative, Anhad, Jan Sangharsh Morcha, Jan Vikas, Citizens for Peace and Justice, The Commonwealth Human Rights Initiative, Foundation for Civil Liberties, Aman Samudaya, Himmat, and many others.

But this work belongs most to the young justice workers and lawyers, and the survivors themselves who have resisted the enterprise of hate and fear by extraordinary acts of compassion and courage. Because of them, I can still hope.

Harsh Mander

Unheard Voices: Stories of Forgotten Lives
Harsh Mander

'An extraordinarily lucid document, speaks to our conscience and makes us think. Each one of the twenty stories is a tale of courage'—*Pioneer*

The Bhopal gas tragedy, the communal carnage of 1984 and 1989 in Delhi and Bhagalpur, the Orissa supercyclone, among others, are part of collective memory. But, often forgotten are those who actually were affected by these happenings, and others like them—street children, sex workers, Dalits, HIV and leprosy patients, the homeless and the famine stricken. These are people who in many ways are pushed to the outermost, most hopeless margins of society in the name of development and progress.

In *Unheard Voices* civil servant and social activist Harsh Mander draws on his own and his colleagues' experiences to explore the lives of twenty such people who have survived and coped despite all odds. Going beyond mere survival, these stories are a testimony of how people have overcome their condition with humbling courage, resilience, and humanism. Marked by understatement and rare warmth, they bring out their determination to seek a better life in the face of enormous suffering. Reaffirming people's creativity and indomitable spirit, this book challenges all those who despair about India.

Non-fiction
Rs 250